COAT POCKET
BIRD BOOK

WRITTEN BY
JOHN GILLETTE

D1547480

ILLUSTRATED BY
DAVID MOHRHARDT

Lansing, Michigan

	DATE DUE		

Table Of Contents

About This Book

This book, and its companion *Kitchen Table Bird Book,* have been published for birdwatchers who want to know more about birds of the Great Lakes region than is found in standard field guides. Two excellent general guides have long been available—Peterson's *Field Guide to Birds East of the Rockies,* and the Golden Press *Birds of North America*—and by working with one or another or both there isn't one single feathered flying body anywhere in our region that's safe from rapid identification. But by their very nature, these field guides are only aimed at providing identification. They have space for only the briefest bits of information about each bird. Peterson depicts more than 1000 birds in the 136 color plates of his book, while the Golden Press contains even more because it covers birds on both sides of the Rockies. There simply isn't room in those books for more than a few words about each bird, plus a small drawing. They are comprehensive, solid reference works, but they include hundreds of birds most of us will never see.

This book, and its *Kitchen Table* companion, march to a different ruffed grouse. They were written to give readers a lot more information about a lot fewer birds—but the birds they do list are those you are most likely to meet in the Great Lakes region without fanatic chase. We make no apologies for not including *all* birds that flap and flit through our region. Together, our two books will introduce you to only about 150 birds. But if you meet and know 90 percent of these, you will find yourself in company with the top 10 percent of those who consider themselves active birdwatchers. And you'll know a lot more about each bird than you'll learn from the field guides, useful as they are.

Arranged By Size

We struggled over how to make this book easy to use. We ruled out trying to arrange the various birds by color, as many contain too many colors. The Blue Jay would be in the blue section and the cardinal in the red section, but where would we place the kestrel, with its red, its white, and its metallic blues? Then we considered arranging them alphabetically, but if you don't know a bird's name, what good is that? Finally, we hit on arrangement by body length, and that seemed to satisfy most requirements for ease of finding in this book the birds you see in the field. They are arranged with the smallest birds in the front pages, moving progressively to larger birds in the back. All you need do is see the bird, guess its body length, and then turn to that area of the book. Once there, flipping a few pages back and forth should bring you in touch with the bird you've just seen. Body lengths are indicated on the plates.

Plumage Changes

Throughout this book, Dave Mohrhardt's paintings depict birds in their spring and summer plumage. Birds molt in the late summer and fall, many becoming very secretive at that time, as though trying to hide their scruffy looks, so birds you do see during that period may be far different from those depicted here. The young ofttimes are also confusing, especially in those species that require more time to reach adult plumage. However, young are commonly seen in company with their parents through the summer, and even into fall for some species, so identification of adults nearby often can provide an answer to both age and family of such youngsters.

Family Groupings

Robert B. Payne's checklist of Michigan birds includes 405 species known to nest in, migrate through, or visit our state. His entire list is included as part of our index material, so you can verify or rule out any birds on which indentification is doubtful. This book contains the 80 most common visitors and residents, which represent 30 of the 60 to 70 families of birds found here. Family groupings divide all birds into units and sub-units based on physical characteristics, food preferences, geographical range, habits, and habitats. Within the professional birding community, wars rage over which birds to include with which groups or subgroups. The two armies are known as *"splitters"* and *"lumpers."* Splitters like to divide birds into more and more sub-units, with decisions usually based on minute differences of plumage or range. Lumpers scoff at this practice, and prefer to lump together into larger groups the sub-units which splitters so carefully establish. I have a friend who has solved this nicely: He makes up his own names for uncertain birds and amuses himself toying with the confusion this causes in hard-line, dead serious birdwatchers. *"Quick, look—there goes a ruby-chested wit-wit,"* he'll snap as a tiny bird flashes out of sight. *"Really?"* says the unwitting companion, *"are you sure? Are they seen here? What? Huh? What do they look like?"* Wits such as this are peppered through our growing bird-watching community these days, so some have to be wary of the traps—especially those of us who struggle with names and nomenclature anyway. A better solution is to take the view of a poet friend who once commented that birds are like large butterflies, while butterflies are like flying flowers. It's an apt description when, on gray wintry days, a tramp afield turns up blue jays, red cardinals, multi-colored kestrels, rusty sparrows, black and white chickadees, and flamboyant grosbeaks. Flying flowers, gardens full of them, on the wing through our lives; that's the way to view these feathered friends.

Use A Pencil

Forget what Mother taught you, this book is meant to be written in, drawn upon, underlined, and otherwise converted from purity to personal companion. Your findings, your personal observations of the colors you see in birds, notes on where you observe individual species, weather, habitat, and other details of the whole movable feast will add to the memory value of this book. Author John Gillette was such a man. He enjoyed his tramps afield, and kept notes on what he saw. Audubon himself was no less a scribbler, nor was Burroughs, nor Leopold, nor any of the host of outstanding American naturalists to whom we all owe measures of gratitude. Gillette died during the course of bringing this book to publication, but not before he left us with his thoughts on the personal and often private sense of meeting that passes between us bird watchers and birds that watch us. His field scribblings are here, converted to whole sentences, and he would be pleased to know that others have taken up this pleasant habit of writing on the pages he penned.

Use Road Kills

We can offer no suggestions on how to prevent birds being killed by cars on the highway, but road kills are, unfortunately, one of the most available sources for identification of birds. A dead bird in the hand allows you to study coloration closely, to measure and comment on feet, bills, tail shape, and other details. Such firsthand study is much more certain than what you may see through binoculars, and the loss of the bird itself is lessened by your bit of knowledge gained. Again, such notes should be added to your copies of these books. However, realize that it is illegal to have songbirds in your possession, either dead or alive, so after taking notes dispose of the carcass.

Finally...

We drew together many individuals to help build this book and its *Kitchen Table* companion, and all contributed with various large dollops of experience and interest. Jim Purvis of Lansing was most steady and determined in his work of rewriting, checking, reworking and collecting necessary elements of the manuscript. Kathryn Breighner of Petoskey reviewed and revised portions of the manuscript at an early stage of the work. John Felsing, our resident bird specialist and a superb bird artist in his own right, provided good sense and direction throughout. Martha McKee, another demon birder, reviewed and rewrote some essays from her perspective as a Wisconsin resident on the west side of Lake Michigan. Incidentally, all of the birds depicted here, so far as we know, are also found in Wisconsin, and most are found in most other parts of the Great Lakes region as well.

As to author John Gillette and artist Dave Mohrhardt—well, they created this book from lifetimes of personal experiences, and creating books is one of life's noble callings. They are therefore noble men, deserving of noble prizes.

Russell McKee
Editor & Publisher

6

The Architecture Of A Bird

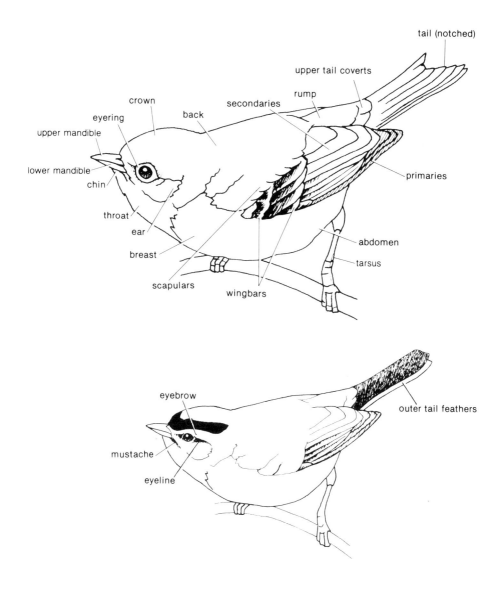

Note: The presence of an eyering and wingbars are two common things to look for when identifying many songbirds. In the illustrations above, you'll note these characteristics are present in the first bird, but are absent in the other.

Winter Wren *Troglodytes troglodytes*

Like a tiny feathered mouse the Winter Wren scurries through brush piles and around the roots of trees growing in the dark recesses of moist forests. It spends its days close to the ground in mossy damp places, often along stream banks, where its dark color and apparently shy behavior make it easily overlooked. When a Winter Wren comes unexpectedly out of hiding, it appears interested in humans and their activities and will spend a good deal of time close by the visitor, its head bobbing as it shares a mutual curiosity.

The Winter Wren is round, dark and dapper, smaller than a House Wren, with a short stubby tail which is usually tipped upward as it hunts forest insects, disappearing under roots, now appearing, in its nervous fidgeting through the deep shadows.

Its stubby upturned tail and heavily barred belly are its best field marks. It is the only wren with dark under parts and dark barred belly. Dark rufous brown above, it has a light line over the eye and a lighter brown breast.

This wren's song is a high tinkling combination of warbles and trills which are long sustained and which end with a high light trill. While its song is delicate, it has been called weird, uncanny, and shrill, but it's always full of variety from robustness to whispers. It is an unexpectedly sweet sound coming often from some dark brush pile along a stream or deep evergreen woods. Its call is an unmusical "*kip kip.*"

But the searcher who is lured into the tangled undergrowth by this wren's song is likely to find the song moving farther away, coming from here and there, and most likely coming from a bird which will not be seen. Possibly because of its ability to stay out of sight, the Winter Wren generally is considered uncommon.

It is called the Winter Wren because this hardy mite often winters in some northern states, though not in ours. It is a summer visitor in the northern half of our state and except during migration it is seldom seen in our southern counties. For those that attempt to winter here, they sometimes fare well where there is open water in streams, but they suffer when the streams freeze and there is deep snow. Its migrations are indistinct because of its wide range in eastern North America. It mainly winters in the Gulf states.

If one is lucky enough to find a Winter Wren's nest, it will be on or near the ground in a recess under tree roots, in a brush pile, under a log or in a tree stump. It is built of fine dead twigs and green moss and lined with feathers and other soft material. The five to seven eggs are creamy white and minutely spotted with reddish brown and lavender.

The young are fed insects and insect larvae, a diet this intriguing bird will pursue throughout its life.

Key Natural History References: Bent 1948, Armstrong 1956.

8

Black-throated Green Warbler

Dendroica virens

Every spring and fall, this yellow-cheeked character is another regular visitor at my birdbath. *The black throat, olive-green crown and white wing bars of the adult male stand out clearly. The white breast has a few streaks dribbling from the black throat.* Females and young birds have duller yellow patches. Light streaks replace the black of the throat on immature birds. Females have dark but mottled throats. Plumages vary so much in the fall that a birdwatcher must look carefully to identify these warblers. Some lack the black throat by autumn but all will still wear the bright yellow triangle mask. This common warbler is smaller than a House Sparrow, about five inches long. Waves of black-throated birds fly across the Gulf of Mexico from the Yucatan peninsula in the spring. Most of them follow a route that is west of Florida, maybe the Mississippi Valley, and come to us about mid-April. Some of them stay in the Appalachians or along the coastline of North and South Carolina, but most go north to the upper Great Lakes, New England and the provinces of Canada to raise a family.

Coniferous stands, usually hemlocks, are the favorite breeding sites of the Black-throated Green Warblers. Cup-like nests are placed on horizontal branches and are carefully concealed in beds of needles. They may be found up to heights of 75 feet in the trees and are compactly built of twigs, moss, bark and feathers. Cowbirds seldom lay eggs in these lofty nests, which probably helps to keep this warbler population at a healthy level. The female lays four or five eggs in the neat cup. Each creamy white egg usually has a heavy wreath of brown at its wide end. Listen for the slow, wheezy *"zoo-zee-zoo-zoo-zee"* of this warbler during nesting.

Incubation by the female lasts 10 to 12 days. The brood is born blind. Their plumage is a fine brown down. For 8 to 10 days the nestlings depend on both parents for their insect diet. This species is not known for snatching insects from the air as the Flycatchers do. They hop and hover over the bark, collecting their meals little by little. On their rich protein diet the young grow quite rapidly, but they do not develop fully colored adult plumage until they return from their first winter in the West Indies.

As October approaches, the black-throated green adults also change colors, as do many of the warblers, making identification difficult. Dusky streaks frame the yellow face during the winter months. By the time they reach us again in April, their golden cheeks will be distinctive.

Key Natural History References: Forbush 1929, Kendeigh 1945, Morse 1976, MacArthur 1958.

Female

Male

Bank Swallow *Riparia riparia*

The Bank Swallow, smallest member of the swallow family, is a gregarious little bird which migrates, feeds, and nests as part of a flock. And the flock, apart from nesting time, often includes other species of swallows. *Here is a graceful, swift-flying bird, a typical swallow, which can be identified most readily by the dark band across its white breast.* The back is a dull gray-brown without any hint of the metallic luster some swallows show. *Its tail is modestly forked, and the sexes are alike in appearance.*

The Bank Swallow is one of two Michigan birds which dig burrows for their nests, the other being the Kingfisher. Literally dozens of Bank Swallows congregate at perpendicular sand or clay bank areas, where they perforate its face with dozens of holes leading into tunnels 1½ to 3 feet long. The hole itself is usually only 1½ x 2½ inches in size and the bank face may be riddled with such holes. In the bulb-shaped end of each tunnel, mated pairs build a simple nest of grass, straw, and feathers.

To the watcher, the burrow digging seems to be a light-hearted task, a characteristic which marks the Bank Swallow's whole outlook on life. It digs with bill and claws, resting on its tail, progressing three or four inches a day. Sand or soil is kicked out by the birds, shuffling backward along the tunnel. As this unique apartment house grows, piles of soft sand or clay accumulate at the base of the bank. Usually the tunnel slopes gently upward with an arched ceiling above a flat floor. Such sloping prevents flooding during rainstorms. Frequent-

ly the task is abandoned as all the workers join together to fly about the bank, feeding on insects and conversing in a soft dry buzz, a sort of *"brrt, brrt."* A flock in unison produces a low, unmusical rattling sound.

By the time serious nesting begins, the whole upper part of the selected bank is fairly honeycombed with Bank Swallow homes. Even though more new burrows are dug than used, old burrows are renovated in succeeding years. While the sheer vertical bank that holds these nests keeps the Bank Swallow secure from predators from below, colonies nevertheless are preyed upon by hunting animals which burrow down from overhead. Still, Bank Swallows are prolific, and usually lay four to five pure white eggs. When the young leave the burrow, the flock is enlarged by many times, and long rows of hungry juveniles, often seen perched on utility lines, are a pleasant noisy climax to the colony's summer efforts.

Bank Swallows feed almost entirely on winged insects which are caught in the air. Occasionally they vary their diet with berries in season. The Bank Swallows, or Sand Martins, or Bank Martins, as some call them, leave our region in the fall, flocking with other swallows for the long trip southward to wintering grounds in South America.

Key Natural History References: Petersen 1955, Graber et al. 1972, Beyer 1938, Bent 1942.

Bank Swallow 4½-5½ inches

Palm Warbler *Dendroica palmarum*

For residents of the Great Lakes region, the Palm Warbler carries a name which doesn't fit. In spring and summer, when its plumage is the brightest, it frequents cool sphagnum moss areas of the north and extends its range far into Canada. That's a long distance from palm trees: and, in fact, even in the winter it is more apt to be found in the saw palmettos of Florida and Louisiana than it is in palm trees.

The Palm Warbler is a tail wagger and the constant up and down motion of that white-spotted balancer is a good means of identification. The sexes are alike in plumage. In the spring, if you see a chestnut-capped ground-feeding tail-wagger, you will most likely be looking at a Palm Warbler. The chestnut cap is less distinct in fall. The bird is yellow from its chin to under its tail, although the belly color varies with the season and its geographical location, from yellow to white to gray. The breast and sides are streaked with reddish brown and rust. Wing bars are lacking or indistinct.

Palm Warblers are found most often on the ground, where they forage for the usual warbler insect fare which they vary in northern parts of our region with various types of wild berries when they are ripe. The Palm Warbler hops about, from bush to bush, or along the ground, as if it were a small Sparrow—and with that tail in nearly constant vertical motion.

Its call is a rapid, buzzy trill, similar to a Chipping Sparrow's or Junco's, which seems to say "*thi, thi, thi, thi, thi.*" During migration the call is a sharp "*chip*" or "*chuck.*"

While the Palm Warbler's nesting range is largely in Canada, it does nest in the northern Great Lakes region as well. The nest is built on a hummock of moss or lichens on the ground at the base of balsam or spruce trees; however, occasionally it is found a few inches above ground in the crotch of a small conifer. The nest is of bark, weed stalks, and dried grass and lined with soft grass, rootlets, and feathers.

An early migrant, the Palm arrives in our state in mid-April ahead of most other warblers. By mid-May the bulk of the migration is moving on into Canada but returns to the state in early September, by then a much duller bird in plumage, to add a few weeks of confusion to the lives of birdwatchers who try to sort out one fall warbler from another. It's a busy task that makes for fall uncertainty and winter conversation, but a gradual growth of understanding of the bright feathery creatures in our midst.

The Palm Warbler winters in Louisiana and Florida and occasionally is seen north along the East Coast to Massachusetts.

Key Natural History References: Forbush 1929, Bent 1953, Walkinshaw and Wolf 1957.

Palm Warbler   4½-5½ inches

Magnolia Warbler *Dendroica magnolia*

This quick, fidgety bright little warbler is one of the most numerous in our state during spring and fall migrations. *It has the attractive habit of spreading its tail to display the broad white band at mid-tail, which is the distinctive marking. It is the only warbler with a broad white band across a black tail.*

The Magnolia is gray and black above with a yellow chest and yellow patch on its back. It has white shoulder patches as well and a black mask. The bright yellow underparts are heavily streaked with black. It is a pretty bird, especially against the dark spruce and fir background of its nesting territory. It is generally considered one of the most beautiful woods warblers. The female is only a little less brilliant than her mate. Both seem aware of their beauty and they will readily display that beauty, with wings drooping and tail spread. In fall and in immature plumage the Magnolia is browner above with fewer streaks on the yellow underparts. The head is gray rather than black, and the eye-ring is quite pronounced.

The Magnolia Warbler brought its name from the deep south where it was observed and named by ornithologist Alexander Wilson, who found this bird migrating through the magnolia trees of Mississippi very early in the 19th Century. After migrating north to nesting grounds each spring, it is mainly seen in the northern portions of our Great Lakes region. It has a variety of songs which are often described as similar to those of various other birds. A Massachusetts observer, listening carefully, phrased one as sounding like: *"she knew she was right, yes she knew she was right"* and *"pretty, pretty Rachel ."*

The Magnolia's diet consists of various insects, which it gleans from tree bark. The nest is at best poorly built and loosely fashioned of twigs, weeds, grass, rootlets and lots of animal hair if it is available, horse hair being preferred. Where there are no horses, fine black roots are substituted. Typically it holds four creamy white eggs boldly marked with chestnut brown and lilac. Magnolias do nest in our state, but only in the northernmost counties. Nests are typically placed in small balsam firs or spruces, and are seldom located more than six to eight feet above ground level.

In the fall the Magnolia Warbler travels all the way to Central America, where it warms its toes through the cold months while its human friends here in the Great Lakes region await the spring return of this bright and friendly migrant.

Key Natural History References: Forbush 1929, Bent 1953, Kendeigh 1945, Morse 1976, Stenger and Falls 1959.

16

Warbling Vireo *Vireo gilvus*

The Warbling Vireo is heard more often than it is seen, for it feeds, nests, and sings high in the branches of deciduous trees where dense leaves shield it from view below. The shade trees it favors are in open woods, along roads, or in shady villages, also in orchards and along river bottoms. It appears to avoid high elevations. This bird is widespread over eastern North America in the summer, and may be common in some locales, uncommon in others.

It sings its song frequently, even while sitting on its nest, a long, warbling and melodious song, containing 12 to 20 notes. It is often called flutelike, and sometimes is compared to a lightly blown bugle call. The notes ripple to a slightly higher note at the end, only to be repeated again and again. A Warbling Vireo, true to its name, will sing its pleasing song, according to one estimate, as many as 4,000 times a day during the breeding season. The male, which shares incubation of the eggs, often sings while on the nest, and as with most birds, only the male sings. This almost constant bubbly spring songfest is one of the best signs that Warbling Vireos are close by.

This is a small gray bird about the size of a Song Sparrow distinguished as a Vireo by a *lack of wing bars,* a lack of other conspicuous markings on any part of its body, and a whitish breast. *There is a faint light eyestripe, but it is not outlined with black as it is on most Vireos.* The general body coloring is pale to medium gray with a slight greenish cast. In spite of its lack of color, *the blunter shape of its bill and slower movements mark it as a Vireo.*

The Warbling Vireo spends its days in search of insects, especially caterpillars, which it picks from leaves and outer twigs in the middle and upper sections of trees, usually near the branch tips.

Here it builds a compact little cup nest of finely woven fiber and strips of bark, grass and cobwebs, lining the whole with fine grass. The nest is placed high, from 20 to 90 feet above ground, on slender horizontal branches. Sometimes, however, a drooping limb will place the nest only a few feet above the ground. The female typically lays four eggs spotted with sepia, umber and reddish-brown. It spends about a month incubating and feeding its single brood each summer.

The Warbling Vireo's range covers much of the United States and Canada. It winters from central Mexico to Guatemala and El Salvador, and arrives in its U.S. and Canadian nesting territory, including most of the eastern U.S. north of Dixie, in April and May.

Key Natural History References: James 1976, Bent 1950.

Blackburnian Warbler *Dendroica fusca*

Birdwatchers never forget their first sight of a Blackburnian. Also known as the "fire throat," in spring the male's flaming orange throat and breast catch the eye at once; he also sports this color on his crown and in an eye line that stretches from his beak to a small orange patch on his shoulder. The rest of his head is black, his back and wings are black streaked with white, and his underparts are off-white. The female is similarly pattern-ed but much duller, as is the male in fall. They are about five inches long.

A deep-woods warbler, Blackbur-nians favor big trees, particularly hemlocks, and spend most of their lives high above the ground. They are a restless and quick-moving bird, though not shy. They will flit from limb to limb in the big trees they love, pausing to preen and look around with rapid turns of their head. They eat in-sects and feed almost entirely on bee-tles, caterpillars, ants, and other forest pests injurious to trees; berries are also consumed when insects are scarce.

Blackburnians almost always nest in coniferous trees—usually hemlocks but also fir, spruce, tamarack, and pine trees—at heights that vary from five to more than eighty feet. In suitable nesting habitats they con-gregate in loosely scattered assemblies almost like a colony. Each nest is built of twigs, plant down, and lichen, well away from the trunk, and lined with hair and fine grass. The four to five eggs are white and marked with vary-ing shades of brown spots sometimes found over the entire surface of the egg but usually formed in a wreath around the large end. Since they make their homes so high off the ground Blackburnians are not often victimized by cowbirds laying eggs in their nests, though a few examples of this have been reported by birdwatchers. Both parents feed the young.

Their song is thin and smooth with two main variations. The simpler one: *"zip zip zip titi tseeeee,"* is almost lan-guidly uttered, while the second one is more hurried and ends on a sharply ascending scale—an explosion of small, crowded notes: *"teetsa teetsa teetsa teetsa zizizizizi"*—somewhat like a Nashville Warbler's song.

The summer range of this bird in-cludes southern Canada, the upper parts of Minnesota, Wisconsin, and Michigan, all of the northeastern United States from Maine to Penn-sylvania, and a narrow strip that ex-tends to take in the Appalachian Mountains. In southern Michigan we're most likely to see Blackburnians during spring and fall migrations; they inhabit the woods of the Upper Penin-sula and northern Lower Peninsula all summer. Winter finds them warming their feathers in Central and South America from Costa Rica to Peru.

Key Natural History References: Bent 1953, Griscom 1957, Kendeigh 1945, Morse 1976, MacArthur 1958.

Female

Male

Blackpoll Warbler *Dendroica striata*

The male Blackpoll Warbler is the *only Warbler with a solid black cap above white cheeks and white throat.* In color, it looks a bit like a Chickadee, but lacks the Chickadee's black throat. It is frequently confused with the Black-and-white Warbler, but the latter's crown is streaked with white and it, too, has a black throat.

Otherwise, the Blackpoll is smoky gray above, spotted black on white below. There are black streaks on the back and sides and white bars on the wings.

The female is quite different, lacking the black cap, and being olive-gray above with buffy white underparts dotted with black. In fall the two sexes appear much alike, both keeping the white wing bars, both being lightly washed with pale yellow, both losing the black belly spots. Pale legs and white under the tail help to identify them. Immature birds also fit the fall description. Both young and adults in fall are dull and indistinctive compared to the brightly marked male in spring breeding plumage.

The Blackpoll is one of the most abundant woods warblers in North America. It arrives in the Great Lakes region in May or June at a time when most other warblers have already moved on to Canada. It is, in fact, our latest arriving warbler, a point that can help in identifications. It is abundant, and prefers treetops to lower limbs.

When they arrive, they have survived a remarkable migratory feat which annually takes a mighty toll of this species. Each fall its migration route to South America takes it out over the Atlantic. Once land is left behind, there's no stopping during a 2300-mile flight to the tropics that takes 86 hours through oxygen-thin air as high as 21,000 feet. The result is a heavy toll of young and weak from sheer exhaustion. Over land, because this bird migrates at night, many also fly into tall buildings and towers.

Since the Blackpoll nests principally in Canada and seldom, if ever, in the Great Lakes region, it is seen here only during migration. In southern parts of our region it is most abundant in fall.

Its call is a thin *"tsit, tsit, tsit, tsit, tsit"* and a deliberate, mechanical *"zi, zi, zi, zi, zi, zi, zi, zi"* given in a single pitch. In migrations its high-pitched calls come out of the darkness from high overhead. The Blackpoll's food is insects, spiders, and larvae gleaned from tree leaves and twigs, or taken on the wing in Flycatcher fashion. It is a valuable aid to man for its ability to attack insect infestations and feed upon them until they are reduced in an area.

Key Natural History References: Bent 1953, Forbush 1929.

Pine Warbler *Dendroica pinus*

As its name suggests, the Pine Warbler prefers to spend its days in open pine woods where it hops up tree trunks and along branches in search of insects and spiders. Its constant gleaning of bark and needles has earned it the nickname "Pine Creeper," and it probably plays a fairly important role in keeping pines clean of insect infestations. It feeds in this manner more than any other yellowish warbler.

The Pine Warbler is dusky yellow above and has a bright yellow throat and breast unstreaked except for occasional faint markings. *The amount of yellow on its underparts varies from bird to bird, but its conspicuous white wing bars, unstreaked back, and white spots on the underside of the tail are distinctive. It also has a yellow eyestripe, white belly and white tail spots.*

The female and immature young can be confused with the Bay-breasted and young Blackpoll Warblers, so the Pine Warbler is best recognized by its pine woods habitat. During migration, however, when the Pine Warbler moves about in orchards and deciduous forests, this similarity makes for difficult identification.

This is not a conspicuous warbler and its preference for singing from the highest branches of large pine trees makes it easily overlooked. However, it is also a tame little bird sometimes seen feeding gracefully on the ground. When disturbed there it flies to the trunk of the nearest tree where it clings like a Brown Creeper. When it hangs from a cluster of needles it reminds one of a Titmouse. It will fly considerable distances from tree to tree and, at times, flycatcher-like, it makes aerial forays after passing insects.

The Pine Warbler's song is a liquid trill, a slower and more musical version of the Chipping Sparrow's song. In addition to insect life picked from tree bark, the Pine Warbler adapts when insects are scarce by eating seeds from sumacs, pines, grasses and berries; also poison ivy, dogwood, Virginia creeper and wild grapes. It can be attracted to bird feeders with a mixture of peanut butter and corn meal.

The Pine Warbler is not a frequent nester here, limiting itself to the upper part of the state and the northern Great Lakes generally. It builds a compact and deeply hollowed nest on a pine branch 10 to 25 feet above ground, using weed stems, bark strips, and pine needles, lining the whole with fern down, hair and feathers. The female usually lays four whitish eggs marked or spotted with a variety of browns.

By fall the Pine Warbler plumage has softened to a plain gray-brown and, with its young fledged and on the wing, is ready for the migration to our southern states and south into the Bahamas and South America.

Key Natural History References: Forbush 1929, Bent 1953.

24

Pine Warbler   5-5½ inches

Prothonotary Warbler *Protonotaria citrea*

The Prothonotary Warbler is a busy flash of gold in the shady lowlands of swamps and flooded woodlands. The name Golden Swamp Warbler, sometimes attached to this bird, more accurately describes it, but the bright yellow plumage reminded Louisiana Creoles many years ago of robes worn by papal scribes. The scientific and most common name is from the Latin for *notary* or *scribe*, the root of Prothonotarious, and so the Golden Swamp Warbler is really still the Prothonotary.

The Prothonotary is the only warbler with a bright golden head free of other markings. It is mostly yellow below with bluish gray wings and tail. Both sexes have similar plumages, and while the female is slightly duller, males and females are almost indistinguishable.

The southern counties of our state mark the northerly limits of its range, where it prefers flooded woodlands and damp swampy river bottoms. There it hunts close to the water, covering every nook and cranny of its territory in minute detail searching for caterpillars, ants, flies, bees, locusts, aquatic insects, spiders, and small snails—all of which it gleans from the trunks and branches of trees. When it occasionally sits motionless, it is usually high in a deciduous tree.

The males return in April, ahead of the females, from their winter in Central and South America. Their first business is to establish a territory by engaging in aggressive battle against other Prothonotary males, as well as chickadees and wrens, until a territory the size of several football fields is clearly defined. Then in a sort of chauvinistic enthusiasm the male builds a nest. But it is a dummy nest, one spurned by the female as soon as she arrives.

The real business of nestbuilding is handled by the female. She chooses a natural cavity in a tree, an abandoned woodpecker hole or a nesting box. The site is usually over water and not far above its surface in a shaded spot. There, she typically lays six beautiful rich creamy or rose-tinted eggs marked with brown and gray. This warbler's song is a rather plain but emphatic *"Tweet, Tweet, Tweet, Tweet, Tweet,"* given in a single pitch and varied with a short metallic *"Pink."*

Because it is protected by its habitat, the Prothonotary Warbler has few enemies except the House Wrens, with which it contends for nesting sites, and from snakes which share the swampy bottomlands and take advantage of the low nesting sites to attack eggs and young.

The favored haunts of this five and one-half inch jewel of a bird are penetrated with difficulty, but it is a foray well worth the trouble when the observer is rewarded with a chance to watch this unusually beautiful and energetic little warbler.

Key Natural History References: Griscom 1957, Walkinshaw 1938 and 1953, Simpson 1969.

Bay-breasted Warbler *Dendroica castanea*

In the fall of 1980, my birdbath accommodated more of these birds than any other migrating species. Some of the Bay-breasted Warblers that bathed had their full quota of russet feathers, but many had barely a trace of brown on the sides of their bodies. Generally, the habitat of this group is away from the thick woods, but they make a temporary stop in my oak-maple woods on migration. They linger in each tree they visit, scouring it for insects with slow, deliberate movements. In breeding season they stick to conifers, stream banks, and fence rows, and will be found from central Canada to northern Minnesota, northeast New York, central Vermont and New Hampshire, and southern Maine.

When the bay-breasted beauties arrive in spring, the males have on their dressiest garb. *A rich chestnut color decorates the crown, upper chest, throat and sides, and a large, buff neck patch can be seen behind the black around the eyes. The back of the bird is gray-brown and the two white wing bars are plain.* Females have duller colors all over the body, and young ones that you see in the fall have an olive-green back with little or no russet feathers.

Nests of the Bay-breasted can be found in conifers rather close to the main trunk of the tree, sometimes as high as 40 feet off the gound. Tightly made of rootlets, grass, twigs, and spider silk, they are intricately woven by both sexes. Colorful darker spots decorate the bluish or greenish-white shells of the clutch of four to seven, typically five eggs. The female sits on the eggs for 12 days and occasionally is fed by the male. The male sings his high-pitched, weak song while he waits for the young to emerge. After the youngsters hatch out, the male helps feed oodles of insects and spiders to the hungry brood. The Bay-breasted is almost exclusively insectivorous, which is quite beneficial to the conifers. In fact, this warbler often feeds on outbreaks of swarming insects, such as spruce budworm infestations.

In August, the new crop of these warblers joins the veterans for a long journey across our southern states, over the Gulf of Mexico and farther on to Panama and the countries in the northwestern corner of South America. There they find plenty of insects, and both sexes put on the beautiful colors that all of them have on their spring trip to breeding territories.

Key Natural History References: Chapman 1907, Forbush 1929, Griscom and Sprunt 1957, Mendall 1937.

Female

Male

Red Crossbill *Loxia curvirostra*

The Red Crossbill is another "winter bird" that comes to the lower Great Lakes states somewhat irregularly. *They are a bit larger than a House Sparrow—about six and one-half inches long—and can be quite friendly. If you can edge close to this bird, be sure to take a good look at its unique bill.* It is a special cross-over style, large for the body size and used for cracking open pine seeds, its favored food in the wilds, plus any other hard seeds you offer it at your feeder. None appeared in our yards during the mild winter of 1979-80, although during past heavier winters we have attracted small numbers of them.

Nesting occurs rather early in spring along the Canadian border in the eastern half of the United States. The pair builds a nest of cedar bark, moss, grass and leaves placed far out on the branches of evergreens. The nests are so well concealed amidst the needles that you may have a hard time locating one. Since the female is a dull olive-gray color, she can sit quietly on a nest and escape detection. The distinctive brick red plumage of the male would not blend with the needles so he just brings her food while she sits. The heavier-billed female has a yellow rump and resembles young Purple Finches without the heavily streaked breast. Notice the blackish wings and tail of the male. The female is noted for staying long periods of time on the nest and probably needs to do this because nesting occurs so early when the weather is still quite chilly.

Four or five young birds emerge from the nest with the color of the female, striped above and below, suggesting a large Pine Siskin, and their bills do not cross until about three weeks of age. Up to the age of about one year, the young males do not show a predominance of red but have a mixture of olive and yellow and some red. Perhaps some of the males never turn as red as many sketches are inclined to show. These winter birds with the heavy beak and short tails will enjoy your sunflower seeds and sit for many minutes in an open feeder filled with them. Some of them stay well into May helping themselves to your hand-outs. Crossbills can be seen clinging to pine cones. You can hear them noisily extracting seeds with their peculiar bills. The bird acts like a small parrot as it dangles from the cone while eating. Be sure to watch carefully for the few white-winged species which may visit our feeders. They will be mixed in the flocks of other birds but can be easily identified by the obvious white wing bars.

The song of the Crossbill is a finch-like warbled *"jip-jip-jip-jeaa-jeaa."* This unpredictable visitor to the Great Lakes states prefers the rich conifer forests of Canada, and generally visits only the northern portions of Minnesota, Wisconsin, Michigan, New York, Vermont, New Hampshire and Maine.

Key Natural History References: Griscom 1937, Lawrence 1949, Bent 1968.

30

Male

Female

Yellow-bellied Flycatcher

Empidonax flaviventris

The Yellow-bellied Flycatcher is easily distinguished from its numerous close fly-catching relatives, many of which look like slightly different versions of the same bird. *The Yellowbelly is different in that it is small, short-tailed, has a distinctly yellow chest and underparts with a greenish back, and has the habit of constantly flicking its tail. It has two white wing bars and a slight eye-ring.* Note that it is little different from its cousins, the Least, Alder or Willow Flycatchers except that it's yellow in the fall. *The Yellowbelly is uniformly yellow over its throat, chest, and belly, all the way back to its tail.*

This sparrow-sized bird spends its summers in the evergreen forests and cold bogs of Canada and the Upper Peninsula. The upper Great Lakes, in fact, is the southern limit of its summer range so this bird is seen farther south only during migrations. In the northern summer, it stays hidden in low growth close to the ground. This secretive nature makes the Yellowbelly a difficult bird to see, but if you think one is nearby it can be coaxed from cover by making a squeaking call. I do this on the back of my hand. Its responding voice is the best identification. The call sounds like *"pse-ck!"* and its descending whistled *"pur-wee"* is unique among flycatchers because most others do not include a whistled song in their repertoire.

Typically, the Yellowbelly catches insects on the wing, but it also eats large numbers of beetles, ants and spiders. In severe weather it can survive by eating the berries of the mountain ash and also wintergreen berries.

This is the only Flycatcher known to nest on the ground. On a mossy knoll or fern-covered bank it sinks its nest of mosses, fern stems, and slender roots right into the ground, bringing the top edge to ground level. Often the nest is roofed over and reached by a short, protected passage making it all but invisible. Eggs are usually three or four in number—rarely five. They are dull white and are sometimes marked with a few small blotches, but more usually are dotted with tiny spots in various shades of brown, grouped around the large end of the egg or scattered over its entire surface. Michigan, however, is not a favorite nesting area and those which breed here are only found in the most northerly portions of our region.

The Yellow-bellied Flycatcher is most often seen passing through in its spring and fall migrations. It moves north from Central America through the central United States and arrives in our region in May when northbound, and is ready to depart southward by August or September.

Key Natural History References: Bent 1942, Walkinshaw 1957.

Semipalmated Sandpiper *Calidris pusilla*
Sanderling *Calidris alba*

The sparrow-sized Semipalmated Sandpiper is perhaps America's most abundant shorebird during migration. It is brownish above, has *a faint wing stripe, black legs, and webbing between its front toes*. The foot is not fully webbed, as in duck feet, and that partial webbing gives this bird its name, "Semipalmated." The sexes are alike in plumage.

These sandpipers are often seen in spring and fall along our Great Lakes beaches in flocks of 20 to 40, twisting and turning in the air with fine precision as they wing along, showing first their dark backs, then their white breasts. When they settle on sand flats or a pebbly shore to feed, they peck at the sand and move about rapidly and aggressively, seeking insects and small crustaceans, their major foods. They work along with heads down, watching especially for beetles, their form of dessert. The call of this bird, given in flight, is a crisp "*cherk*," or "*chi-up*."

They are often seen asleep in bunches along an upper shore, each bird standing on one leg, head tucked under wing. If you approach too closely, they'll try to hop away on one foot; if you move even closer, they'll reluctantly put down the other leg and peddle off.

The Sanderling is somewhat larger, but still smaller than a robin. It is a rusty brown bird with a white belly, black bill and dusky primary wing feathers. In fall, when migrating south through our region, it becomes whiter below and grayer above. It generally is the palest and whitest of the sandpipers. In flight, *it shows a long, white wing stripe on top, angled in a V-shape and running outward from the body almost to the wingtip. When precision-flying as compact flocks, these birds are seen as being light-bodied with dark wings, the upper wing stripe being clearly visible*. When feeding, they chase retreating waves, running pell-mell down the beach to water's edge, then turn and dash back out of the way of the next wave. As they run, they poke the sand and peck at tiny snails and other crustaceans or water insects momentarily exposed by the wave. It rarely is seen on upper, drier parts of the beach, but it can be approached closely near the water when feeding. Its call is a snappy "*quick-quick*." They do not move about in large bunches, frequently feeding alone or in pairs or small groups.

Both the Semipalmated Sandpiper and the Sanderling nest on the Arctic tundra far north of our region. Sanderlings winter in South America as far south as Chile, a distance of 8000 miles from their nesting site. The winter range of the Semipalmate is broader, extending from some coastal areas of the eastern United States south through the Gulf states and into South America. Both birds are seen in the Great Lakes region mainly in the middle weeks of May, and again in the early fall just traveling through.

Key Natural History References, both birds: Pough 1951, Bent 1962, Payne 1983.

Semipalmated Sandpiper (top)   5½-6½ inches

Sanderling (bottom)   7-8 inches

Vesper Sparrow *Pooecetes gramineus*

The Vesper Sparrow was named for its evening song, for it sings from sunset to dark, a time when most other birds have ceased for the day. But it sings, too, throughout the day even in the heat of summer midday. It is, in fact, one of Michigan's most dedicated songsters during late spring and early summer. Its simple songs begin with two clear whistled notes followed by two higher ones, ending with short descending trills. It sings on the ground, from perches, and even when flushed from its nest.

Because of its preference for dry, grassy fields and because of its mid-summer singing, the Vesper Sparrow brings thoughts of hot dry days. Even its appearance adds to the impression; it is gray-brown and evenly streaked over upper body and undersides. *It is distinguished from other sparrows by white outer tail feathers and a chestnut colored patch at the bend of its wings*. It looks warm on a warm day. Perched, it also looks somewhat like a Song Sparrow, although it has a white eye-ring and no breast spot.

Adding to its apparent preference for dryness is the Vesper's fondness for dust and frequent dust baths. Where there are flat dirt roads you will often find Vesper Sparrows dusting on summer days. It rests in "dust puddles" in the shade, or nearby under large-leaved weeds such as mullien. A constant water supply for drinking or bathing does not seem to be a Vesper Sparrow requirement, and it has no apparent objection to flying some distance for water.

This sparrow is a dedicated nester and is often still attending to family raising after most other birds have finished for the summer. It raises two broods each year, sometimes three, building its nest in open land where the grass is not too long. The nest is made of weed stalks and grasses sunk into a hollow scratched out of the ground so deeply that the upper edge of the nest is often flush with the surface. There the female lays three to five, usually four, bluish or pink-white eggs spotted with brown, purple and some black. The nest most often is found at the base of a grass hummock, and early in the season may be quite exposed until surrounding vegetation grows up to conceal it.

As would be expected from its dry open habitat, the Vesper Sparrow feeds mainly on grass and weed seeds, varying its diet with insects and grasshoppers. It gathers these foods by gleaning, and one study showed the diet consisted of one-third insects and two-thirds vegetable matter.

In October it begins its fall migration to Florida and the Gulf States, although in the southern edges of our Great Lakes region it will linger until November. In March and April it returns to our state when watchers once again can listen for its brilliant song, often heard best on calm evenings and on the clear air after spring rains.

Key Natural History References: Bent 1968, Wiens 1969, Bryant 1931.

Piping Plover *Charadrius melodus*

The chances are good that, even with casual birdwatching, you will see most of the birds in this book. They were selected because they are frequently seen in Michigan.

The exception is the Piping Plover.

Once common along the Great Lakes shoreline, the Piping Plover is now a rarity.

Only 31 pairs were noted in 1979, 16 in 1981 and just 12 pairs were recorded in 1982. They are no longer seen along Lakes Erie and Ontario, and it took the accumulated shorelines of Lakes Superior, Huron and Michigan to produce the last 12 pairs.

In his 1912 book *Michigan Bird Life* Walter Barrows wrote that "this little plover is found everywhere along the shores of the Great Lakes during summer..." He called it common.

In the years since many field birds which were rare then have made strong comebacks and are commonly seen now, primarily because of conservation laws and an enlightened public. But not the Piping Plover. Why?

One reason is that Michigan's Great Lakes beaches, which attract this plover, also attract people in increasing numbers. They use the beaches not only for sunning and bathing but also as race courses for offroad vehicles which devastate the nests of this little shorebird.

A renewed effort by the Audubon Society, the Nature Conservancy and the Department of Natural Resources to protect the Piping Plover's habitat accounts for this bird being included in this volume.

If you should be fortunate enough to sight a Piping Plover, you will see a little (6-7½ inches) whitish shorebird the color of dry sand with a black ring around its neck. Since it blends so well with the beach color, it is very difficult to pick out unless it moves.

Its back is sandy gray; its underparts white and there is much white on its head. The narrow black band above the forehead is not unique to this species, but *the black neck band is the best means of identification.* The bird illustrated here has a complete band, but most Piping Plovers will show either an incomplete or a very narrow band. The bill is short, typical in plovers, and is yellow with a black tip.

When feeding, it behaves much like a robin, running a short distance before stopping to stare at the sand with its head slightly tipped to one side, then picking up the tiny bits of animal life it finds there.

It has a twisting, turning flight, during which it gives the melodious, clear *"peep peep peep lo"* whistle which gives it its name.

The Piping Plover is a pale version of its close relative the Semipalmated Plover. It is, really, a small insignificant bird, one which is easily overlooked both literally and in our priorities of threatened species. But should it disappear completely from our shores, Michigan's out-of-doors will be much the less for it.

Key Natural History References: Pough 1951, Jurek and Leach 1977, Bent 1929.

Semipalmated Plover *Charadrius semipalmatus*

The Semipalmated Plover looks like a Killdeer although it's only half to two-thirds its size. It wears a single black collar—and so is known also as the Ringneck or Ring-necked Plover—while the Killdeer wears two.

Over-all the Semipalmated is dark brown above, the color of wet sand or mud. Against a sand or mud background it has a protective camouflage which serves it as well as if it were hiding among rocks or in deep grass. It has a white tail, white face markings and a white throat and collar which accent its black collar. *The single black collar and the muddy brown back are its best field marks.*

In flight in small compact flocks it demonstrates a finely developed syncronization as the birds twist and turn in perfect unison with each other. As many as 40 or 50 birds will form a flock, but each twist and turn made is as if a single mind were dictating it. Some believe the responsibility is the lead bird's, while others believe their observations tell them that the command, if it is that, passes down the outside of the flock as different birds take turns passing along some signal known to the others but still a mystery to man. How the plovers perform this aerial ballet is still one of those many secrets birds have not given up.

On the beach when feeding it runs with its head erect, pausing from time to time as if a thought had suddenly struck it, then bending to pick at the sand for tiny morsels of aquatic food. Inland it searches freshly plowed fields for earthworms and insects and is a natural enemy of the grasshopper, which it consumes in large numbers.

Nests are a mere depression in the sand, without lining or with only a few bits of shell or grass to form a rough outline. The three or four eggs are buff to brown in color, spotted with blotches of black or very dark brown. The young leave the nest and run after the parents almost as soon as they are hatched. When danger approaches they will often imitate adult behavior by standing or lying motionless on the sand, making it almost impossible to see them.

The Semipalmated Plover nests far north of Michigan in Canada, however, so the best chances of observing it come in the late summer and early fall as it begins a four-month leisurely migration which eventually takes it to the Gulf of Mexico. It's seen mainly along the beaches of the Great Lakes.

A single call note, a *"cherk"* or *"chur-wee"* comprises the Semipalmated's verbal message to the world. It is as sparse as the Black-bellied Plover's single, shirred whistle, a ringing *"pee-u-wee"*.

Key Natural History References: Peterson 1980, Bent 1962.

Yellow-breasted Chat *Icteria virens*

The Yellow-breasted Chat is a member of the warbler family, but is an unwarbler-like bird in a number of ways. Almost as large as a Catbird, it has a large unwarbler-like bill and behaves in a manner uniquely its own and not at all in the way of most woods warblers.

Its best field marks are the white spectacles and bright yellow breast seen in both sexes. The upper parts are olive green, the lower belly is white, and there are no wing bars. The long tail gives the impression of being a bit loosely fitted together.

While the Yellow-breasted Chat is fairly common throughout the Great Lakes region during the warm months, especially in the more southerly portions, it is a master at avoiding observation, and so is heard more often than seen.

Its peculiar song, which you may hear coming from the depth of thickets and the dense undergrowth of deciduous forests, is an odd assortment of whistles, caws, mews, toots and clucks. Clear whistles alternate with harsh notes and soft Crow-like caws. Sputters, cackles, and whispers interrupted by loud whistles do little to remind one of a typically melodious warbler song.

Occasionally the Yellowbreast imitates other birds, and it has some reputation as a ventriloquist. Sometimes it sings on clear moonlit nights, or even in near total darkness, and *its habit of singing on the wing over dense cover, head thrust downward and legs dangling, marks its most frequent sightings.* There is also a distinctive, single call note which has been described variously as a *"whoit"* or *"kook."*

While the Chat stays out of sight if it knows it is not alone, it will reward the patient watcher who sits quietly, for at times it will hop onto a branch in plain sight and begin its loony repertoire or fly off in its clownish head-down, legs-hanging, tail-pumping flight, singing all the while. At such times it seems truly an eccentric bird.

The Yellowbreast nests in low bushes or tangles of briars or vines where it builds a cup of grasses and leaves, lined with finer grass roots and, at times, hair. There the female lays three to five white or pinkish eggs which are spotted with brown and gray.

The Chat's diet is largely insects—beetles, bugs, ants, wasps, bees and caterpillars. When fruit is in season it appears to be fond of wild strawberries and blackberries.

In early fall the Chat begins its long migration to Central America where it remains until the spring flight north, which brings it back to our region for the May nesting season.

Key Natural History References: Forbush 1929, Bent 1953, Thompson and Nolan 1973.

43

Common Screech Owl *Otus asio*

The cry of the Common Screech Owl, heard only at night, can almost bring tears to human eyes. Anything but a screech, it is a mournful, plaintive, quavering wail, sounding like a lost soul somewhere in the darkness. A resourceful birdwatcher can imitate the call by tilting the head back and whistling through saliva on the end of the tongue. And the imitation may be rewarded with an answer and may draw the owl into flashlight range.

If you do see one, the light will reveal *a robin-sized puff of feathers with yellow eyes and ear tufts. It is the only small owl with "ears."* Its color will be either over-all gray or over-all rich rusty-brown, one or the other. A mating pair may be mixed, one gray the other reddish-brown. Whichever it is, the Screech Owl will retain that color for life. The color appears to be independent of age, sex, habitat or brood. A pair of the same color phase may have a brood of the other color phase. Whichever color it is, the individual bird is uniformly colored over its head and body—all gray or all reddish-brown. Gray Screech Owls outnumber reddish-brown ones about four to one in Michigan.

This courageous, almost savage "feathered wildcat" spends its days quietly in tree cavities or in dense foliage waiting for night. If discovered in its hiding place during the day, it remains motionless, extending its body upward so that it looks like a stub rising out of the limb. At night it flies off to hunt, depending upon its exceptional eyesight in poor light to help in the search for food. It feeds mostly on small mammals, mice particularly, plus a few small birds and large insects, and it is especially fond of crayfish. It also makes up for winter's poor hunting by raiding roosts of English Sparrows, which may be one reason it is frequently seen in and around towns during the cold months, the gathering places of such birds. Moderately common over the eastern United States, it is a year-round resident in our state, though it is seldom heard or seen in the northern counties.

Its small size does not exempt the Screech Owl from the hatred and harassment that Crows and Jays like to visit on owls. They will torment any and all owls whenever they find the daytime roost, and their raucous uproar is a standard signal to birdwatchers that an owl has been found and may then be seen in its hiding place.

Pairs of Screech Owls usually mate for life and often return to the same nesting cavity year after year, where this normally tidy bird nests in a clutter of "pellets" and debris of former meals. The pellets are the undigestible remains of mice or birds—bones and fur—which owls typically regurgitate as firm little lumps. Actually there is no nest as such, because the five or six eggs are laid directly on the bottom of the nesting cavity, a tree hole which the pair may have preempted from a flicker. When suitable cavities are not available, the Screech Owl can occasionally be attracted to nest in a birdhouse.

Key Natural History References: Bent 1938, Van Camp and Henny 1975, Earhart and Johnson 1970.

gray phase

red phase

Spotted Sandpiper *Actitis macularia*

The Spotted Sandpiper is hard to separate from Michigan summers, from warm days, and the feel of beach sand under bare feet. The Spotted is our most common Sandpiper, and it is found on nearly every lake around the state, and inland on most streams. Where seen, it teeters along, almost always alone or in pairs, delicately picking at insects and bits of tiny animal life. *This little shorebird is the only shorebird which in summer has large, dark round or irregular spots on a white breast.* Its undersides are marked very much like a Wood Thrush's. It is olive-brown above and has a dark line through its eyes. In flight it shows white wing bars. In fall and winter and in immature plumage there are no spots, but white shoulder marks are distinctive. *Also, the teetering up and down of its body and tail between steps give the impression of delicate balance on reedy little legs.* So the Spotted Sandpiper is known as the "Tip-up" just as some call it the "Peep" because of its call.

When walkers follow it along a shoreline, this little bird maintains a respectable lead, watching as it feeds. When the follower draws too near, it flies on ahead 40 or 50 yards, usually low out over the water, returning to the shore to land. When this repeated pattern carries it too far from its starting point, it will fly out over the water in a wide arc back to where it apparently wanted to be. This casual, routine flight from danger is unhurried and quietly deliberate.

In flight this Sandpiper's wings beat downward, never going above the plane of its body. Such flight is interspersed with brief intervals of soaring. The call is a high clear whistled *"Pee weet. Peet. Pee-weet-weet-weet."*

The Spotted Sandpiper's diet is largely small aquatic animal life and insects. As it runs along the water's edge, hunting with head down, it stops every few feet to inspect and take the tiny morsels which in the aggregate support its active movements. It feeds until late evening and into the early darkness, enough to be considered a bit nocturnal in its habits.

Nesting takes place on the ground and not always near water. The nest may be well constructed or just a few grass stems. Eggs are four in number, buff colored and spotted with black and brown or purplish gray.

The Spotted Sandpiper is common throughout the Great Lakes region from early May to mid-September. It spends its winters in the southernmost edges of the United States below South Carolina, westward to Louisiana and southward into South America.

Key Natural History References: Miller and Miller 1948, Bent 1929, Hays 1972.

Solitary Sandpiper *Tringa solitaria*

A bird of the wooded wilderness, the Solitary Sandpiper spends much of its time in our region beside those watery little woodland pools and quiet little pockets of standing water in the tangles of cedar swamps. Despite being a sandpiper, don't look for it along open beaches for it normally is far inland in the silent depths of the woods.

As its name signifies, it is a solitary bird, almost always alone or with only its mate. It is a slender shorebird as graceful as a swallow in flight and one which *habitually and constantly nods its head.*

The Solitary Sandpiper is olive-brown above and white below, as are others in its family, but it is *unique in its barred white sides with the white extending into the tail. It lacks wing stripes, but has a white eye-ring. The white of its sides and tail are flashy and especially conspicuous in flight.* There is no spotting on the undersides. Another identification aid is the fact that its back is darker than most Sandpipers' and its *legs are long and dark colored where others are yellowish.* A mature bird measures seven to nine and a half inches in body length, slightly smaller than a robin.

When standing quietly the Solitary Sandpiper will jerk its head and body stiffly upward and back in a sort of spasm, as if it were suffering from hiccoughs. As it runs, it bobs both head and tail. If you flush a Solitary Sandpiper from the edge of a woodland pool, you'll be surprised to see it fly swiftly upward, at a sharp angle, on deep steady wing strokes, sometimes until it is several hundred feet overhead, then flutter downward and return directly to the place it has just left. As it flies it gives a sharp whistle composed of three or four *"peet"* notes, a sort of *"peet-weet-weet."*

It was not until the 1920s that the nest of the Solitary was first accurately identified. In fact, it does not build its own nest. Because it lives in woodlands surrounded by other birds, it leaves nest-building tasks to Grackles, Blackbirds, Cedar Waxwings, Robins, Kingbirds and jays and uses their old nests. Unlike other sandpipers, therefore, it is a tree nesting bird. Its four eggs are greenish white and heavily spotted with reddish brown.

In the forest ponds it calls home, the Solitary finds aquatic insects, small mollusks and land insects. It hunts the aquatics by wading and gently stirring the pond bottom with its feet.

Winters are spent in the tropics of Central and South America. The Solitary returns to Michigan in late April, disappears from its normal haunts in June, and then returns in July where it remains until September.

Key Natural History Reference:
Bent 1929.

48

Sora *Porzana carolina*

The Sora runs through the dense marsh grass like a little bantam hen, sometimes zipping lightly over lily pads and sometimes making short, weak flights in its steady search for food. It is a common marsh bird here in the Great Lakes region during warm months, but one which is seldom seen because of its secretive habits and ability to disappear quickly into its grassy surroundings. Also, much of its activity takes place at night.

A small gray bird hardly as large as a robin, *the Sora, or Sora Rail, is distinguished easily by its short, thick yellow bill which looks as if it should belong to a chicken rather than a Rail. Its small, narrow, but round body is barred on the flanks and marked with a black patch on face and throat.* Immature birds are buff colored. Supposedly, "thin as a rail" refers to this bird, a body shape that allows easy transit through dense marsh grasses.

Look for Soras on the edges of ponds among cattails, reeds and marsh grass. Even when there is no hint that one is around, most potholes and sloughs probably have at least one pair. Toss a stone into the marsh edge and you will often get a response of Sora calls. A descending whinny-like call is characteristic, and in spring a rising "*kee-wee*" whistle may mark the hiding place. The call is a sharp "*kee*." All in all, the Sora is a noisy bird, but even so its dull coloring and ability to stand motionless make it difficult to locate.

Its search for food produces insects, snails, and floating aquatic seeds, but three-quarters of its diet is composed of above-water plant seeds. It especially likes wild rice.

The nest will usually contain 8 to 10 buffy white eggs heavily spotted with brown and purple. However, the clutch will sometimes number twice that many, requiring two-story housing to get all eggs beneath the sitting parent. All these are laid in a little platform nest of dry grass built on vegetation growing from water a few inches below. Green grass overhead is often pulled together in a sort of protective arch and serves the birdwatcher as a signal that a nest is underneath.

In spite of its seemingly weak flight, the Sora is migratory, and when the first frosty nights of fall hit our region, the Soras are up on the wing and off to the south, flying low, in bunches, and at night. Its migratory flights, which can carry it over the Caribbean, are often 3000 miles in length. It winters in the southern United States, on islands in the Caribbean, and south to South America.

In marshlands populated with long-legged Herons and splashing water-birds, seeing this dainty little puff walking matter-of-factly through tall grass makes a day of tramping and mosquito swatting well rewarded.

Key Natural History References: Odum 1977, Tanner and Hendrickson 1956, Bent 1926, Webster 1964, Walkinshaw 1940.

50

Sora

8-9¾ inches

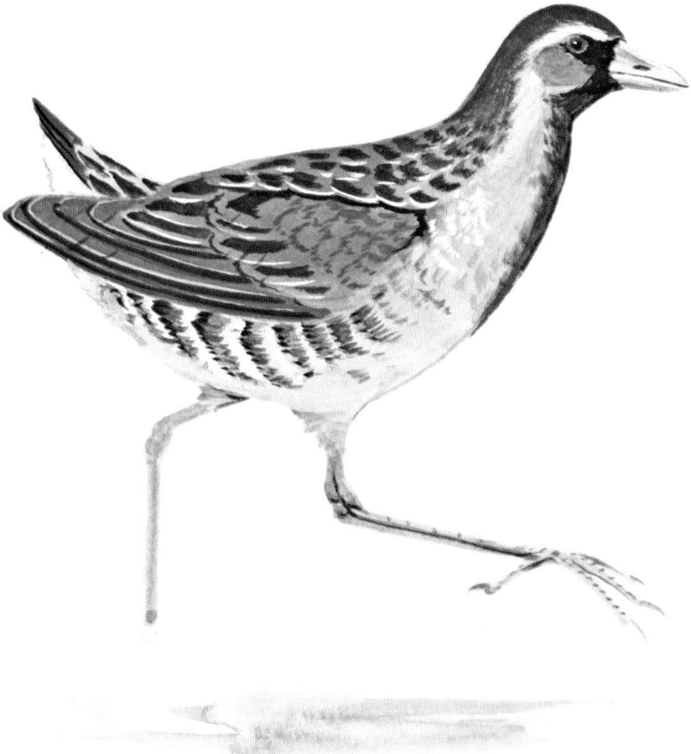

Common Bobwhite *Colinus virginianus*

Its call is one of the cheeriest sounds in nature. After a summer rain the Bobwhite's bright *"bob-white, bob-bob-white"* rings across farmlands and open fields as liquid clear as the rain-washed air, a sort of audible rainbow which makes any early evening a richer experience.

A chunky "miniature chicken" about the size of a Meadowlark, and found in the same habitat as the Meadowlark, the Bobwhite is a ground feeder and nester. Its flights are rapid, short, and they usually end in long glides.

The Bobwhite is reddish brown and has both a short bill and a short dark gray tail, giving it altogether a somewhat rounded appearance. The male is strikingly marked with a white throat and a white band which extends across the forehead through the eyes and down the sides of its neck. These same areas are buff in the female. Both are a handsome mottled brown and white on the sides and underparts.

The Bobwhite is a favorite with birdwatchers, farmers, and hunters. The latter two groups are inclined to call it "Quail," which it is, even though it calls its name *"bob-white"* repeatedly from fence post perches. In recent decades its numbers have grown sufficiently in our state to make a limited hunting season possible. Protective coloring and explosive flight make it a popular, challenging game bird.

Numbers vary from year to year, for the Bobwhite is quite susceptible to winter kill when deep snows cover its food and the gravel it needs for digestion. It sleeps in small flocks called coveys, the birds grouped in a ring, heads turned outward, ready for instant flight. These concentrated groupings sometimes perish as a unit when freezing rain or driven snow covers them. The southern Great Lakes region is the northern edge of this bird's range. But nevertheless, this is a durable, hardy little bird which thrives on a summer diet of insects and survives on seeds during the winter.

In May or June it begins nesting and often has a second brood of young if the first fails through some mishap.

The nest is well hidden, often in a bower of deep grass. The female lays a phenomenal number of small white eggs, from 10 to 24, which, when hatched, will form a family group or covey which stays together even after the young are grown.

Sometimes, if you are walking across a field at dusk or just after dark, such a covey will scare the daylights out of you by exploding into wild flight, in all directions, from right underfoot. Next morning, there will be a lot of *"bob-white," "bob, bob-white"* calling heard in the area, as the little family unit attempts to gather itself together again.

Key Natural History References: Bent 1932, Rosene 1969, Stoddard 1931.

Bobwhite   8½-10½ inches

Female

Male

Eastern Meadowlark *Sturnella magna*

Every spring it is a recurring pleasure to hear meadowlarks proclaim their presence in the open fields of our area. These birds return to us early from the southern United States and perch on telephone poles and wires along our country roads. They are common in the Lower Peninsula, less so in the Upper. *Eastern Meadowlarks have a bright yellow breast with a black V-shaped stripe just under the throat, and are about the size of a robin with a shortened tail. Look for the very plain white tail feathers as they fly across the field; their backs are streaked brown.* They stay out of the woods where I live, preferring to live in open fields and meadows.

Males oftentimes mate with several females, and the females receive no help from the males in building their ground nests. Nests are made in three to eight days of grass and weeds and many of them have a roof; the roofed ones have a side entrance. The nests are well hidden, but occasionally a tiny path may be found leading to the nest through the vegetation in the immediate area. After she completes the nest, the female lays about five whitish eggs with light spots on the eggshell, and sits on them for nearly two weeks. After they are hatched both parents feed the young, although the male contributes much less than the female. By the 11th or 12th day the young leave the nest and test their wings by taking short jumps and fluttering briefly over the grass. They are still fed by the parents for at least two more weeks. Since the Eastern Meadowlark raises two broods each season, the female soon gets busy making a second nest, sometimes starting it only two or three days after her young desert the first one. While she is building and laying this second time she continues to feed the first brood, but when the second incubation begins the male assumes the major part of the work of caring for them.

When you see the large bill of this species it makes it rather hard to believe that their summer diet is mostly insects. This bird does a lot to control the population of the larger insects such as grasshoppers. In winter, fields of Texas, New Mexico, and other southern states are saturated with meadowlarks but not to the point of being a nuisance. I've seen many of them in these states, but they are not gregarious like the blackbirds.

From March through August the song of the meadowlark can be heard ringing across Michigan's open fields. It consists of two clear slurred whistles: *"tee-yah, tee-yair,"* the last note descending. This cheery yellow-breasted bird is a welcome visitor to our rural areas each summer; look and listen for him in March as the dragged-out days of winter begin to fade.

Key Natural History References: Lanyon 1957, Roseberry and Klimstra 1970, Bent 1958.

Northern Shrike *Lanius excubitor*
Loggerhead Shrike *Lanius ludovicianus*

They look like Mockingbirds in their black, gray and white plumage, but there the similarity ends. No rollicking singers in magnolias, the Northern and Loggerhead Shrikes have earned the name of "butcherbirds" for their diet of small birds, mice, snakes and insects, and for their habit of impaling prey on thorns or barbed wire, or for wedging it securely in branch forks to be eaten later at leisure.

Both the Northern and the Loggerhead Shrikes are fairly uncommon in the Great Lakes region. In winter the watcher may see the Northerns anywhere in the Great Lakes region as they wander sporadically as lone individuals. In summer, it's the Loggerhead we see, but only in the southern counties of the state which are the northern limits of its summer range. *Each is about the size of a robin, gray above, white below with black wings, tails and a mask-like eye streak. The Northern has faint barring marks on its breast, and the lower mandible is yellow, while that of the Loggerhead is black.*

Shrikes are most commonly seen on the topmost branches of tall, dead trees or perched, tails parallel to the ground, on telephone wires where they watch for prey with keen eyesight. They can see bumblebees at 100 yards and small birds at twice that distance.

Not having the speed and killing capabilities of hawks, they sometimes stalk their prey by flying close to the ground, sometimes by hovering until a mouse exposes itself, sometimes by pursuing fleeing birds and insects with great precision and determination.

They seize their prey with beak and feet all at once, usually killing quickly with sharp, quick bites behind the head. In spite of folktales that they torture their prey, the Shrikes' victims are usually dead before being impaled on thorn or wire. However, you may someday find a single haw or thorn-apple tree hung with the limp bodies of large insects, mice or small sparrows, a larder which takes on the look of an old-time butcher shop. When you do, you will know it's the lair of a shrike. The diet is mostly large insects, with mice, voles and small birds making up about twenty-five percent of the total volume.

The Loggerhead Shrike nests early in our state, often before mid-April. The nest is a large bulky affair of twigs set deep within a thorny bush. As many as six or seven eggs are laid in each of two nests during the nesting season.

In October most Loggerheads leave for the southern states; a few stay behind to winter in Michigan's southernmost counties. Northern Shrikes are winter visitors seen most commonly in the Upper Peninsula and in Berrien County at the southern end of Lake Michigan.

Key Natural History References, Northern Shrike: Cade 1967, Miller 1931, Bent 1950.
Key Natural History References, Loggerhead Shrike: Graber et al. 1973, Miller 1931, Bent 1950.

Northern Shrike   (top)   9-10 inches
Loggerhead Shrike   (bottom)   9 inches

Black Tern *Chlidonias niger*

The Black Tern is robin-sized. It has a black body with the black extending up the neck and on to the top of its head. Its wings are gray, its bill black. *This is the only black-bodied Michigan tern, but it has white on its head, neck and breast. The tail is notched rather than forked.*

In many respects, the Black Tern looks like a Purple Martin, and its scientific name, in fact, translates roughly to "black swallow."

This is the Black Tern in spring breeding plumage. However, by mid-summer when the adults begin to molt into winter plumage, with heads and underparts turning a patchy black and white, *they are best recognized by their short, notched tail.*

In fall and winter the head is white with a black nape, the back is still dark and the tail is gray. This is the bird's appearance on its long fall migration down the Mississippi flyway and along the coasts to Central and South America.

The Black Tern's role as an "aquatic swallow" extends to its diet of insects which it snatches from the air. In flight the Black Tern seems as light as a butterfly, and its darting, zigzag path when chasing insects suggests a flycatcher or a nighthawk. Watching on hovering wings, it will also swoop down to take grasshoppers, beetles and a variety of winged insects from tall grass. Mollusks, crayfish, spiders and other invertebrates are also included in its diet.

It nests in loose colonies in mid-June on or close to the marshes which are its most common habitat. The nest is sometimes quite elaborate and well made, but more often it is just a loose cup of reeds sufficient to keep its three olive or buff eggs from rolling into the water. Occasionally nests are placed on pieces of driftwood or boards where they are very conspicuous, but usually they are very hard to see. It's usually not hard to find a Black Tern's nest, however, because these little birds are among the boldest when it comes to driving off intruders, and their defensive maneuvers will reveal the locations of their otherwise well concealed homes. These fierce defenders of their nests and young will attack the curious in angry swoops, occasionally striking a stinging blow on a person's head.

In their second summer the young, which are still in a white-breasted phase, seldom come north with the breeding adults, remaining in the deep south nearer their winter range.

The Black's flight call is a sharp *"keek, keek, keek,"* but in those attacks on intruders near its nest the call becomes a shrill screamed *"Kreek,"* a warning to leave.

Key Natural History References:
Peterson 1980, Bent 1963.

58

Killdeer *Charadrius vociferus*

"**K**illdee, killdee," this graceful shorebird calls as it wings away from the walker, fluttering only a few feet above the ground. It is restless and noisy and can be seen as readily over expanses of paved parking lots as over gravelly shores, and on the open plowed fields of the countryside.

The Killdeer is one of our earliest spring birds here in the Great Lakes region and the best known of the family of plovers. It is often seen far inland from the water. It is not difficult to see because it is so often in motion and because its plumage is so striking and bright. About ten inches long, it is olive brown above and pure white below. *There are four black bands on the body, two on the head and two on the breast.* Its rump is a bright orange-brown and in flight the long wings show a white V-shaped mark.

Every country school boy has seen two of the Killdeer's most notable characteristics. These involve its nesting habits and the protection of its young. The nest amounts to practically nothing, just a spot on pebbly ground where sometimes a few small stones are pushed or pulled into a circle, within which four eggs thickly spotted with brown and sepia are laid. Usually, too, the nest is in an open field where approaching intruders are easily seen, but sometimes it is on the gravel alongside a highway and occasionally even on the gravelled roof of a building. The young are precocial and able to scurry for cover as soon as they are outside the egg and sun dried.

When humans or predators approach the nest or young, they are treated to an exhibition of dramatics and anguish by the parent bird which almost invariably dupes the intruder into leaving the threatened area. *The parent performs a broken wing act, using one wing folded over its back and the other dragged helplessly on the ground*, an act marked with accompanying piteous cries. All this is done just a few feet ahead of the pursuer. The fox intent on an easy kill, or the human lured into being a good Samaritan, is led away to a safe distance where the parent suddenly flies off, taunting the follower with sharp cries of *"killdee, killdee."* Meanwhile, the vulnerable young, left far behind, have frozen into motionless invisibility, looking for all the world like little pebbles themselves.

In courtship the male flies back and forth over a field giving its loud, but sweet, call for as long as an hour. When joined by the female, the pair will fly high into the sky, then drop suddenly to just above the ground where they will repeat the activity.

The Killdeer is one of spring's first birds and one of Michigan's last birds to fly south—a characteristic which multiplies the pleasures of knowing it. The Killdeer winters from the south central United States into Columbia and as far south as Peru in South America.

Key Natural History References: Bent 1929, Pough 1951, Nickell 1943.

American Kestrel *Falco sparverius*

The American Kestrel or Sparrow Hawk is such a pretty, light-hearted little fellow it has inspired writers to poetic heights in describing it. "The prettiest and jauntiest of our hawks, yet no prig," one wrote. Another called it the "most light-hearted and frolicsome" of all hawks.

That the Kestrel has colorful plumage no one can deny. *It is the only falcon with a rusty red back, and the male's blue-gray wings are distinctive. Both sexes have two black mustaches or whisker markings on either side of the head, adding to the jaunty dress.*

The Kestrel is one of Michigan's most common hawks, and the smallest member of the hawk family, being about the same size as a Robin. It is a familiar sight along highways year around, where it sits hunched up on utility wires or fence posts, intently watching the ground below—for grasshoppers and crickets in summer, and mice or English Sparrows in winter. When its sharp eyes spot prey, it swoops after it with great speed on long pointed wings. At other times, you'll see it along highways hovering 15 to 30 feet above ground, wings moving rapidly to hold it in place, as it surveys the mice below.

When disturbed it will fly off a short distance, hover in one spot, then return to the same perch when the threat has passed. If you see such action, just keep moving and watch what happens. *This ability to hover is a good field mark, because the Kestrel is the only small hawk which does it.* Some larger hawks hover, but the Kestrel is only the size of a Robin.

The species is Swallow-like in flight and a small model of the Falcon clan with large head, broad shoulders and long pointed wings and tail.

Kestrels apparently mate for life. Their nests are built in tree cavities or old Woodpecker holes—which it sometimes preempts—and nesting boxes or building enclosures from six to fifteen feet above ground. There it lays from two to five white eggs thickly speckled with cinnamon brown.

Insects are the staples of the Kestrel's diet. It is especially fond of grasshoppers, crickets, and beetles, but the diet is varied with mice, shrews, small birds, reptiles and amphibians being included. Surplus food is commonly cached against days when the hunting is poor.

Occasionally the Kestrel is wrongly identified as being a Pigeon, or a Sharp-shinned Hawk and, surprisingly, as a Mourning Dove because of the latter's similar size and habit of sitting on utility wires. But the Kestrel's sharp *"killy-killy-killy"* or *"klee-klee-klee"* call, the two sometimes intermixed, adds to this bird's air of light-heartedness, and also to its general impression of being quite business-like in its war on pests.

Key Natural History References: Bent 1938, Roest 1957, Smith et al. 1972, Balgooyen 1976, Willoughby and Kape 1964.

Male

Common Nighthawk *Chordeiles minor*

The best time to see a Nighthawk is in the evening as it wheels through the darkening sky in pursuit of insects. After dark, its nasal loud *"peent"* comes from overhead, and on warm summer evenings it flashes through the upward glow of street lights on main streets all over eastern North America, including the Great Lakes region.

The Nighthawk is often confused with the Whip-poor-will. Both are members of the Goatsucker family, a name given by superstitious Europeans who once believed that such birds visited pastures at night and stole milk from grazing goats. Both Nighthawks and Whip-poor-wills are nocturnal in varying degrees. Both also are brown, dead-leaf in color, and robin sized, with long bent wings.

But the two are easily distinguished. *The mottled gray-brown Nighthawk has a white patch across its wing and a patch of white across its tail and on its throat. In flight it resembles an over-sized swallow with a forked tail and a bounding, erratic course interrupted by fast wing beats.* The wings are long and pointed and bend backward, and when folded at rest they reach to the end of the tail.

The Nighthawk has a peculiar habit of roosting lengthwise on branches and perching diagonally on wires. The Nighthawk generally prefers open country, but is perhaps seen most often in towns and villages. In the country, it nests in open fields or on rocks; in town nesting occurs frequently on the graveled roofs of buildings, where two to four eggs are laid on the roof itself, without use of padding such as grass, feathers, or sticks.

A spectacular bird, the Nighthawk has acquired some colorful nicknames which give hints to its appearance and habits. "Bull Bat" refers to its nocturnal habits, and "Mosquito Hawk" was acquired both because it looks a little like other hawks and because it feeds on flying insects. The insect diet is taken mostly on the wing although the bird seems to enjoy ants and sometimes hunts insects on the ground.

The Nighthawk is also the author of a unique sound which booms down from the darkened skies and is a part of its courtship behaviour. Flying to great heights, it suddenly dives at great speed toward the earth, checking its speed with outspread wings and tail a mere few feet above the ground. This sudden mid-air braking produces a deep humming sound as passing air rushes over wing feathers. The sound has been variously described as "blowing over a barrel bunghole" or a "feathered Bronx cheer." It can be an unsettling sound to one who doesn't know about it beforehand. The performance, and the sound, will be repeated over and over into the spring evening.

In fall, Nighthawks grown fat on insects migrate southward where, in the 19th Century, they were targets for hunters. Their numbers diminished at an alarming rate around the turn of the century, but protection has since made this bird a common and favorite sight for Michigan birdwatchers after sundown.

Key Natural History References: Bent 1940, Armstrong 1965.

Whip-poor-will *Caprimulgus vociferus*

"**W***hip-poor-Will, Whip-poor-Will, Whip-poor-Will!*" Imagine that threat to poor Will being loudly called outside your bedroom window several hundred times without interruption, hour after hour, night after night. You would know this Michigan night bird well—perhaps too well—even though you might never see it.

If your disturbed sleep finally drives you into the outdoors, flashlight in hand, you might catch a glimpse of a broad-winged bird flying noiseless as a moth to another favorite perch, perhaps on the tool-house roof, or off to a favorite fence corner. With luck, the flashlight would reveal a bird about the size of a robin with large round eyes which reflect cherry red in the light beam. Even when disturbed to a new location, it continues the emphatic and well known *"Whip-poor-Will"* calling, preceding each with a barely audible *"chuck"* and a deep bow of its head on the first syllable.

That is about all anyone ever sees of the Whip-poor-will, a Michigan member of the Goatsucker family (see Nighthawk for the explanation of this unusual family name). Preferring wooded areas, the Whip-poor-will spends its days perched lengthwise on a limb or among dead leaves on the ground where its dead leaf color makes it practically invisible. It is heard throughout the Great Lakes region in the summer.

It has mottled brown plumage with a black throat. *The male has white on the sides of his tail and a white band beneath the black throat. His mate is all brown, the throat band being buff colored.* Other notable features of the Whip-poor-will are *an immense mouth and bristly "whiskers" which extend beyond the end of its small bill.*

This ghostly bird lives largely on moths and flying beetles which, through great aerial acrobatics, it catches on the wing. Since its feet are small and weak, the Whip-poor-will seldom feeds on the ground. But it nests on the ground, on dead leaves or decayed bits of wood beneath underbrush, without bothering to build a nest as such. There it lays two white eggs marked with spots of brown, yellowish brown, and lilac. When disturbed, the nesting bird, like the Killdeer, feigns injury to distract intruders and lead them from the nest area.

The call which gives this bird its name can, indeed, be persistent. It is given 50 to 65 times a minute, often without any interruption for 100 to 200 calls. Pauses between these marathon series are often short-lived. The naturalist John Burroughs told of counting 1188 "blows laid on poor Will's back" before a half-minute pause, followed by another series of 390. Burroughs couldn't sleep either.

Fortunately this call is usually muted by distance because its owner is a deep woods bird. But to Whip-poor-will fanciers, the two happiest nights of the year are the night of the first Whip-poor-will's call in the spring, and the last one in the fall.

The Whip-poor-will winters in the Gulf states, and south into Mexico.

Key Natural History References: Bent 1940, Raynor 1941.

Lesser Yellowlegs *Tringa flavipes*
Greater Yellowlegs *Tringa melanoleuca*

Size is the main difference between these two long-legged sandpipers. Both are slim-bodied and long necked *with bright yellow legs*. Both are dark gray above with white underparts speckled with dark gray-brown. In flight they appear to be dark-winged shorebirds with white tails and rumps and no wing stripes.

Greater Yellowlegs, at 13 to 15 inches in body length, are the larger of the two and have the subtle distinction of a slightly upturned bill, plus a more wary attitude toward their surroundings, and a habit of swinging their bills from side to side when standing in the water. They sometimes walk with their whole body bobbing up and down.

Lesser Yellowlegs measure 9½ to 11 inches in body length, have a slim straight bill, and are more commonly seen in large loose flocks. They are the more common of the two and are less wary than their larger counterpart.

Both are members of an informal group of shorebirds known as Tattlers, a name derived from their role as alarm sounders. While Greater Yellowlegs can be called and brought to a decoy, they are quick to give alarm once the deception is discovered; Lesser Yellowlegs share this trait. They fly swiftly, both birds capable of speeds up to 45 miles an hour. *In flight, their long pointed wings and long necks and bills are fully extended, and their legs trail out straight behind.* This flight appearance, too, is distinctive. They land with wings extended upward and make a few jerky bows, as if getting their necks back in joint, before returning to gleaning the beach.

Both species feed in shallow water, though not necessarily on Great Lakes beaches. They also pick insects and snails out of rain pools or wet grassy areas, and sometimes feed inland in mowed fields as well. Both are transients seen here commonly during spring and fall migration, though occasionally during summer as well. Lesser Yellowlegs have recently been recorded several times in counties near the Straits of Mackinac during the summer.

Aside from size difference, the Yellowlegs' calls are their best means of identification. The Greater's call is three or four whistles—*"whe-u, whe-u, whe-u,"* and the call is loud and penetrating. In spring its rolling *"whee-oodle"* is repeated. The Lesser's call on the other hand is softer, more nasal, and usually confined to one or two *"cu,"* or *"whe-u"* notes.

Yellowlegs arrive in Michigan in April on their way to the Canadian muskeg nesting grounds, far to the north. They can be seen here until the end of May and can be expected to return from the north in July, to remain until August or September when the Lesser Yellowlegs head for Florida, the Gulf Coast, and South America to winter, while Greaters stop along our Florida and Gulf Coasts for the cold months.

Key Natural History References, both birds: Bent 1962, Pough 1951, Payne 1983.

Lesser Yellowlegs   10-11 inches

Greater Yellowlegs   14 inches

Black-bellied Plover *Pluvialis squatarola*

The Black-bellied Plover is seen in our state only in spring and fall, and *it has a black belly only in the spring*. By fall, this migrant has lost all that dark coloration and is then a mottled light brown and white, more consistent with other Plovers.

Its cousin, the Lesser Golden Plover, also has a black belly in the spring, but that bird migrates northward across the plains and prairies west of the Mississippi river, so we don't see it here. By fall, the Golden has also lost its black coloration and at that time it's very similar to the fall-plumage Blackbelly.

Except for a rare accidental, then, if you see a plover-like bird with a black chest and underparts, and its *in our state in the spring*, that bird is almost certainly a Black-bellied Plover.

By fall, however, confusion reigns, because the Blackbelly and the Golden look so much alike and both migrate southward through our state at about the same time. By then, both have lost their black chests and both are a mottled gray-brown with lighter underparts. The Golden is a bit smaller and darker, and has no white bars in its wings.

The Blackbelly seems to be a bird which is always in a hurry, for on the wing it is one of the swiftest fliers to visit our region. Flight speeds up to 50 miles an hour have been clocked, and its powerful pointed wings beat as rapidly as four strokes a second. It is exceptionally streamlined and fast.

The Blackbelly is the largest of our Plovers, about a foot in body length over-all with a wingspread twice that. *Its stocky build and short, stout bill*

help to distinguish this bird from the other plainer grayer shorebirds commonly seen here in the Great Lakes region in the fall.

It also can run swiftly along a beach when it elects not to fly, and is so mobile and athletic it swims gull-like over puddles of water which get in its way. Its call is a plaintive slurred whistle, a ringing *"Pee-u-wee, pee-u-wee."*

Once considered a prime game bird, the Blackbelly suffered heavily before the guns of 19th Century hunters, especially the spring hunters, and for a period of time its numbers were badly diminished. But its natural wariness and swift flight helped it respond to protection and happily it is no longer counted among the threatened species.

The Black-bellied Plover's southward migration begins quite early and by mid-August the last birds have left their Arctic Circle breeding grounds and have arrived on their southward migration through Michigan.

They will remain here until mid-autumn and then fly on to the south in sizeable flocks, moving along high in the sky, similar to flights of ducks heading to their wintering grounds. However, this bird migrates not only to our southern states, but also continues on to the West Indies, to Mexico, and even to Argentina and Chile in South America.

Key Natural History Reference:
Bent 1929.

Summer

Common Snipe *Capella gallinago*

The Common Snipe, or Jacksnipe, or Wilson's Snipe is the will-o-the-wisp of the marshlands. As it rises suddenly from the marsh grass in its erratic zigzag flight, it seems to be crying *"escape, escape"* in a rasping voice. This sound, really closer to *"scaipe, scaipe, scaipe"* is one of its best identifications. Also known as the Wilson's Snipe, this shorebird is about 11 inches in body length, with a long, slender bill. *It is a brown bird—about the color of dead reeds and, as a result, when hugging the ground and relying on its protective coloration, it is extremely hard to see. The crown of its head is striped, as is its back. In flight it reveals a brown rump and short orange tail.*

The Snipe likes boggy marshes and stream margins where the bird searcher might confuse it with two other species—the Woodcock and the Dowitcher. However, the Woodcock has a large squarish head, huge eyes, and is a chunkier bird. The Dowitcher is more inclined to feed in the open and has less brown in its plumage, with a whitish rump. In short, the *Snipe is best identified by its zigzag flight, the "scaipe, scaipe" call, and its sudden appearance in moist habitat*, where it uses its long bill to probe the mud for earthworms, its principal food. It also hunts for leeches, grasshoppers, locusts, mosquitoes, insect larvae and some plant seeds. When disturbed on its breeding ground, the Snipe has a call described as *"wheat, wheat, wheat."* This call might lead the searcher to its nest in a dry clump of grass, usually hidden under overhanging grasses or bushes. Here the female lays four brownish, burnt-umber blotched eggs.

The elusive here-and-there flight which traditionally has made the bird a favorite challenge to autumn hunters changes to a more direct flight over long expanses of marsh. Occasionally it rises high into the sky. High flights, in fact, are part of the Snipe's remarkable courtship performance each spring. Part of this activity includes flights of high wide circles carried on for several minutes while making a loud, penetrating humming sound, caused by air rushing past the outer wing and tail feathers. Following this circling, there's a sudden dive to about 50 feet above the ground where the flyer then appears to collapse and tumble to *just* above the ground. Just before a disastrous crash, it rights itself and rises sharply to repeat the performance all over again. Finally, it drops into the grass. In more normal flight, however, the Snipe lands in much the same manner: by diving toward the ground, then fluttering the last few feet into the grass.

Look for this interesting bird to arrive in the early spring, as soon as the ground is soft enough to begin probing the marsh for its favorite food, earthworms.

The Snipe nests and summers throughout the Great Lakes region, but winters from the southern United States to Brazil.

Key Natural History References: Tuck 1972, Fogarty and Arnold 1977, White and Harris 1966, Erickson 1941.

Snipe 11 inches

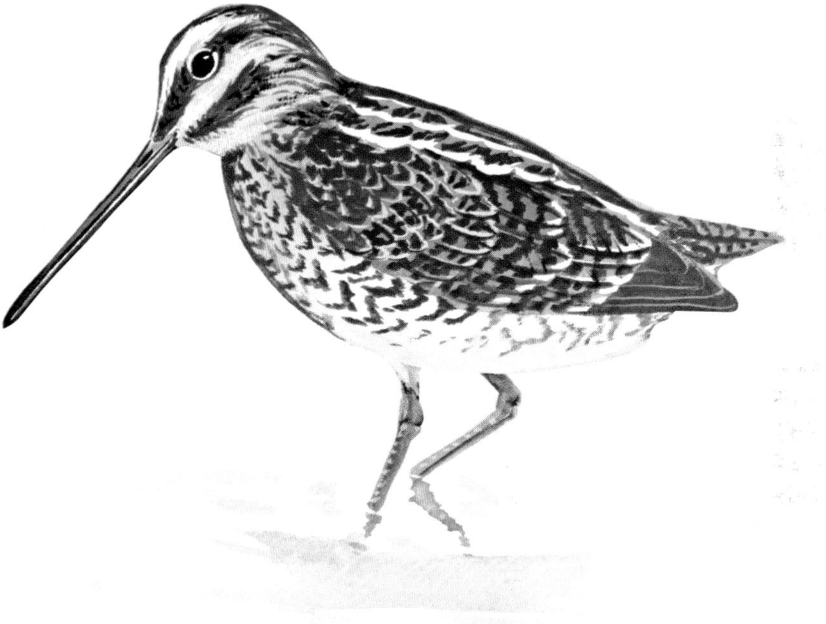

American Woodcock *Philohela minor*

The "Timberdoodle" may be your unsuspected near neighbor. It spends its days on the ground where its protective coloration keeps it well hidden, making it possible for one to stare directly at the bird and not see it resting on dry leaves six to eight feet away.

But finding one is well worth the search and, once flushed, the distinctive corkscrew flight and "scape" call tell you that you have found one of nature's most interesting birds.

The Woodcock is about the size of a Bobwhite, and is dressed in mottled shades of brown, black and buff. *The black and buff barred head is large and squarish with large eyes placed high up and far back on the head. The bill is long with a flexible tip. The legs are short and feathered to the knees.*

The position of the eyes and the nature of the bill are adapted to this little game bird's preoccupation with hunting earthworms. In fact, this bird's total diet consists of earthworms, and many hunters bypass the Woodcock because of its distinctive "livery" taste.

Its food is found by prodding its long beak deep into soft earth, usually in low, moist areas where the flexible tip of the top mandible can be opened and closed to feel for and clasp earthworms, while the large eyes watch for danger from both sides and the rear. A Woodcock may eat half its weight in earthworms in a single night, their preferred feeding time.

The Woodcock's nest is made on the ground in a simple depression of leaves, where three to four buffy eggs thickly spotted with pale rust are laid. If the nest is disturbed, the mother may fly off to a new location, carrying her chicks one by one, held between her thighs.

Another of the Woodcock's remarkable activities is the one which might bring it to the attention of the observer more readily than any other: the courtship performance of early spring. Carried out at dusk, the performance begins with the male strutting stiff legged, on the ground, head tilted downward, calling a raspy *"peent"*, before flying suddenly into the air straight upward 50 to 100 feet where he hovers momentarily, singing a fluid *"chicaree, chicaree"* song. At song's end, he plummets earthward on a zigzag falling leaf course accompanied by a soft *whee, whee, whee* sound of moving wings. Inches before crashing, the little performer rights himself and lands nimbly on the same spot from which he started his flight.

The distinctive calls of the Woodcock, which arrive here in the lakes states from the southern United States, usually by April, are as sure and welcome a sign of early spring as the first robins in the treetops. It is a common summer resident in the Great Lakes region, and winters in the Gulf States and Florida, and along the Eastern Shore as far north as Maryland.

Key Natural History References: Owen 1977, Sheldon 1967, Mendall and Aldous 1943, Bent 1929.

Gray Jay *Perisoreus canadensis*

Throughout the northern Great Lakes region, the Gray Jay goes by a variety of nicknames which suggest its familiarity with humans, and its interesting habits. It is "Whiskey Jack," "Meat Bird," and "Camp Robber" to list the most common. Whiskey Jack probably is a corruption of the Indian name "*wiss-ka-chon*" and was not brought on by any habit of the bird. The other names suggest that it is not altogether a model citizen. Nevertheless, this curious, interesting bird is a winter favorite in our northern woodlands. Formerly known as the Canada Jay, its color has earned it the new name of "Gray Jay."

Although there are a few permanent residents in the Upper Peninsula and on Isle Royale, most Michigan Gray Jays are winter visitors from Canada. They seldom nest in our state, preferring instead to return to Canada before spring to nest and raise their young while there is still snow on the ground. The nests are usually unseen in dense fir forests or tamarack swamps where three or four young are raised. The juveniles are sooty-headed and much darker than the adults. This Jay, about the same size as its colorful cousin, the Blue Jay, is *recognized by its over-all gray color, darker above and lighter below, and by its white forehead, the black patch on the nape of its neck, and the black stripe above the eyes*. In general it reminds one of a large ruffled chickadee.

Hunters, campers, and woodsworkers know the Gray Jay best. It appears from out of the woods, flitting noiselessly from branch to branch as it accompanies a person through the woods. It is furtive and curious. It seldom makes long flights, more often gliding from a treetop to a lower branch in another tree, moving to the top of that tree by long hops and short wing lifts, then gliding on to the next tree. It also appears at the sound of a chain saw or axe, watching and waiting, for it soon learns that where there is human activity there also are easy meals and interesting objects to carry off and examine—a bright bit of aluminum foil, a short piece of tent rope, a lost button. Mostly, however, this bird is attracted readily to a house or camp by table scraps which it carries off to eat or cache in the woods. The presence of food and tolerant humans makes this Jay quite tame and bold as it watches for chances to seize anything that appears edible. Almost omniverous, its summer diet includes insects, grasshoppers, bees, wasps, caterpillars, larvae, and some fruit. In winter, when such food is scarce, it has been observed stealing freshly excavated grubs from smaller woodpeckers.

The Gray Jay has a mixed vocabulary of squawks, squeals, whistles and clucks, plus Blue Jay-like screams. Although it is also a mimic of other birds, its "*whee-ah*" or "*whee-oo,*" softly given, is uniquely its own. The friendly mischievous Gray Jay brings a brightness to dull winter days in our northern Great Lakes woodlands, a joy which contrasts with the dullness of its plumage.

Key Natural History References: Bent 1946, Goodwin 1976, Lawrence 1947.

Upland Sandpiper *Bartramia longicauda*

The Upland Sandpiper is clothed in soft browns and over-all flecks of light and dark markings. *The observer can best rely on body shape and habitat to make an accurate identification.*

Generally it is larger than a robin, or the Killdeer, which it resembles in habit and habitat. *It has a fairly long thin neck, a long tail, and a small head which supports a middling long slender bill.* Its back is a bit darker brown, its underparts paler. The crown of its head and the primary wing feathers are a bit darker than the rest of the back.

The Upland Sandpiper has experienced some name changes, whether it knows this or not. At one time it was called Bartram's Sandpiper, and more recently it was known as the Upland Plover. But it is not a plover, and the present name, Upland Sandpiper, appears most appropriate and will probably stick. Whatever the name, it prefers open pastures and broad flat prairies rather than the lake shores where its cousins, the other Sandpipers, are found most frequently. It is not a water bird, and water is not the place to look for it. It is most numerous in the northern two-thirds of the state.

Over open fields it flies slowly and evenly on wings which seem to be vibrating, for it holds its wings rigid and tilted downward, making it appear to be using only the wingtips rather than the whole wing. Its drifting flight ends in a colorful manner as it checks its speed suddenly and drops lightly to the ground. *After it lands it gives a pretty little demonstration of stretching its wings into the air for a moment before folding them carefully against its body. This habit is a good identification mark.*

The Upland Sandpiper is often seen perched in some high open place which provides a good view of the surrounding countryside. It is not unusual to see an Upland Sandpiper on a utility wire or pole top.

The open fields, of course, produce its food—grasshoppers, locusts, crickets, weevils, and other insects. It mixes this diet with the seeds of weeds as well.

Humans have not been kind to the Upland Sandpiper. Because of its preference for open country it was once an easy bird to hunt, and shooting reduced its numbers drastically. However, as with so many other birds nowadays, its population has increased under protective laws that exempt it from being hunted in our region.

The Upland Sandpiper's voice is musical and flutelike, a sort of mellow whistle that produces a trilled *"gua-'ily,"* a note which has led some to call it the Quaily. Its alarm note is a rapid, but liquid *"quip-ip-ip-ip."* The nest is made on the ground where in late May the female deposits four buffy-pinkish, or pale olive eggs.

In September the Upland Sandpiper leaves the fields of the Great Lakes region for its long flight to the Pampas of South America, returning here usually in April.

Key Natural History References: Bent 1929, Buss and Hawkins 1939.

Common Gallinule *Gallinula chloropus*

Look for the Common Gallinule in marshes and along lake edges of the southern half of our Great Lakes region, where this slate colored bird may be seen swimming in shallow water or wading in the reeds. It frequently is seen feeding close to dense marsh foliage where it can hide if disturbed.

The surest identifying mark is its yellow-tipped crimson bill. The upper face and forehead are also bright red, a shield in shape similar to the Coot's white face. In fact, the two species—Coots and Gallinules—are frequent neighbors. *There is also a white streak along the sides of the Gallinule's body and a dark patch on the top of the tail which is white beneath. The immature Gallinule lacks the bright red bill and face shield.* The Gallinule is easily distinguished from ducks by this shield and by its yellow-tipped chicken bill. Ducks have webbed feet; the Gallinule's toes are lobed—that is, the toes are separate but have wide flaps of flesh on each side. When it swims, this hen-like bird pumps its head and neck back and forth in a rhythm with its feet. Gallinules may frequently be seen bathing and preening. They are a day bird, staying close to the water or marsh edge where they have favorite well traveled paths through the grass. But when they fly, their natural ground-level grace seems to fail them and they appear ungainly and labored. They feed mainly on insects, some seeds, and such other vegetable matter as their habitat produces.

Fledgling Gallinules come in varying sizes because incubation begins as soon as the first egg is laid on the dry reed platform nest. Egg laying and incubation then continues until the last egg is laid and hatched which means that the youngest member of the brood will be a week to ten days younger than the oldest. Sometimes the nest is built like a raft, so it can rise and fall with changing water levels. Sometimes it's placed on dry land at the water's edge. From six to twelve buff-white eggs, sparsely spotted with brown, are laid.

This "water chicken," which early guide books called the "Florida Gallinule," has an assortment of chicken-like grunts, squawks and clucks as well as a complaining "*cak-cak-cak-cak*" in its repertoire of calls. It is a noisy bird, especially during courtship when its nervous *"ticket-ticket"* sound is characteristic.

The Gallinule arrives on its spring breeding grounds from its winter refuge in the southern United States in April and early May. By no means limited in its range to the United States, this member of the Rail family is found as well in South America, Eurasia and Africa and has a close relative in Australia. An awkward appearing bird, the Gallinule is, nevertheless, successful in maintaining its population levels despite civilization, pollution, and loss of habitat.

Key Natural History References: Bent 1926, Strohmeyer 1977, Fredrickson 1971.

Pied-billed Grebe *Podilymbus podiceps*

The Pied-billed Grebe is a favorite companion of summer boys who prowl along the edges of country ponds, both because it is so common and because its nickname, "Helldiver," describes this water bird's ability to dive instantly, leaving hardly a ripple on the water's surface. This Grebe in fact is seldom seen in flight, for it depends upon quick total dives and an ability to submerge part or nearly all of its body and either swim or remain motionless with just its head or the tip of its bill and eyes above water. In this way, surrounded by water grass or among spatterdock, the Grebe can observe without being observed.

The Dabchick or Water Witch, to use its other common names, is a gray-brown bird about half the size of a Mallard duck. It has a thick chicken-like bill. *In summer the light-colored bill is ringed with black, providing the observer with the best mark of field identification.* It also has a black throat patch during the warm months it spends in our region, plus a white rump visible when it swims high in the water. Young birds lack the black ring around the bill and the black throat, but have white striped heads.

Although a water bird, the Pied-billed Grebe has lobed rather than webbed toes to aid in swimming. When forced to take off, it patters along the water, literally running over the surface until it has speed enough to be airborne.

The nest is difficult to reach and easy to overlook. A floating platform of vegetation gathered from the pond bottom, in which the female lays five to eight white eggs, the nest is always carefully covered with nesting material whenever the incubating female leaves to feed. As a result, the vacant nest looks like any other mass of floating pond debris.

The Grebe's diet consists of small fish, plant seeds, aquatic insects, snails and leeches. This combination produces a bird which is worthless as human food, having the taste and smell of a government envelope.

While a highly secretive bird, the Piedbill's call is no secret. It's a raucous, loud *"cow-cow-cow-cow-cow-cowk-cowk"* which rings out suddenly from hidden places around a pond. It is strong enough that much larger birds would be proud to own it. And when its territory is threatened, this Grebe is not shy. A larger duck, alighting in its territory, can be startled into flight at the sight of this compact brown submarine approaching at full speed, half submerged, rising higher and higher as it heads directly for the intruder.

Besides giving small boys free opportunity to use a swear word, the Helldiver is a reliable (though we hope unused) target as well, often moving silently among the water plants when no other birds are found on the pond.

Piedbills leave our region during December, January, and February for warmer weather in the southern United States, but return as soon as warm days unlock local ponds.

Key Natural History References: Bent 1919, Palmer 1962, Forbush 1929, Faaborg 1976.

Belted Kingfisher *Megaceryle alcyon*

A visit to a pond or riverside anywhere in the Great Lakes region will usually produce a Kingfisher; and its performance, watched for awhile, always makes the visit worthwhile. It flies over the water with an uneven wingbeat, pouring out its high rattling call. Then it will hang in midair on rapidly beating wings 10 or 15 feet above the water, its body angled slightly upward as it watches for fish. Suddenly, it will hurl itself full-speed straight down into the water, emerging a moment later with a fish held sideways in its beak. The observer soon recognizes that the Belted Kingfisher is surely a highly-successful angler.

The Belted Kingfisher measures about 12 inches in body length, is blue-gray above and white below. It has a *heavy black two-inch bill, an unkempt upright head crest, and a banded breast. The crest makes it look as though it hasn't combed its hair. The male has a single blue band across its chest, its mate a blue band plus another of rust color which crosses the breast and extends down the sides.* And both have those high scruffy crests. When they launch into their uneven flight, the crest gives them a large-headed appearance, while the tail is remarkably short. Taken altogether, the Belted Kingfisher is a robustly handsome bird.

Basically a fish-eater, the Kingfisher shows an alert intensity that signals the excitement of its chase, although it varies its diet with frogs, crayfish, and some insects. The fish are normally minnows, chubs, and rough fish which come into shallow warmer water, and probably trout are seldom taken, despite what some sportsmen seem to believe. With remarkable eyesight, the Kingfisher spots small fish swimming near the surface, and it is not unusual to see it start a dive by falling directly from a perch high above the water, wings folded. The dive is headlong and uncompromising, and this feathered harpoon hits the water with a smack. When it emerges it usually has a fish, either speared or held in its strong bill. The prey is carried to a perch where it is beaten against a limb to kill it. Then it is flipped into the air and taken head first down the bird's throat. The meal completed, the hunter rattles its satisfaction and flies off to begin again.

The Kingfisher's nesting habits are no less unique. Like the Bank Swallow, it excavates a tunnel 4 to 15 feet long in a vertical clay bank, where it lays five to eight eggs on the floor at the end of the tunnel. The male and female take turns with the incubating, changing off rather formally every 24 hours or so.

Kingfishers arrive from the south in the spring, as soon as open water permits fishing, and leave in the fall only when ice begins to prohibit it.

In ancient times this bird was called the Halcyon. It was this bird which gave the name to the "Halcyon days of summer" when the weather is most pleasant and the waters most calm.

Key Natural History References: Cornwell 1963, Bent 1940, White 1953, Sayler and Lagler 1946.

Male

Female

Bufflehead *Bucephala albeola*
Common Goldeneye *Bucephala clangula*

These two ducks, basically both being black and white in plumage, are common cold weather ducks in our region. The Common Goldeneye is a lingering winter visitor, while the Bufflehead migrates through the state in early spring and late fall. Both may be seen on cold-running streams and on patches of open lake water at those times. The Goldeneye is the larger of the two, measuring from 18½ to 23 inches in body length. The male has a green-black head with *a round white spot between the bill and eye*. Otherwise the back is black, the underparts white, and the wings show a white patch. The female has a more grayish body and no cheek spot. The Goldeneye is a shy bird, usually seen in small flocks that fly off quickly on human approach, wings beating so rapidly they make the whistling sound which has earned it the nickname "Whistler." Its quickness also earned it the name "Spirit Duck" among early hunters because it could dive to safety as soon as it saw the muzzle flash of those old market hunter shotguns.

The Bufflehead—short for Buffalohead, so named because of its large puffy head—similarly has a dark back, white underparts, and white wing patch on the male. The distinguishing mark is *the large white patch which covers the back of the entire head. In flight the Goldeneye looks as though it has a large white eye; if most of the back of the head is white, it's probably a Bufflehead*. The female Bufflehead is brown, has a small white wing patch and a somewhat smaller, but still distinctive white head patch. The Bufflehead is a smaller duck, only 14 to 15 inches in body length. It arrives here fat as a butterball each fall and can be seen on bays and inland waters from October to December. It winters in the southern U.S. generally, though some remain over winter in open water as far north as the southernmost counties of our state. Most, however, head south, to return here in March and April. Its fall plumpness, incidentally, earns it the nickname "Butterball."

Common Goldeneyes and Buffleheads are similar in their habits. Both are shallow water divers, both are fast flying, both escape as often by diving as by flying. They congregate in small, random bunches on the water and often the species intermingle.

For bird-starved winter watchers the Goldeneye and Bufflehead offer a colorful sight at times when most field birds are warming their bottoms in southern states, or are difficult to find and see because of winter conditions. They dash recklessly up and down winter rivers or bob on icy black waters, their dressy black and white plumage contrasting sharply with their winter-dulled surroundings. And, lucky for them, their tough, fishy flesh gives them low marks as game for duck hunters.

Key Natural History References, Common Goldeneye: Carter 1958, Prince 1968, Bellrose 1976, Palmer 1976 v.3. Key Natural History References, Bufflehead: Erskine 1971, Palmer 1976 v. 3, Bellrose 1976.

Bufflehead (top) 13-15 inches

Goldeneye (bottom) 20 inches

Female

Male

Female

Male

American Coot *Fulica americana*

The Coot is an amusing bird which moves over the waters of shallow ponds with its head bobbing like a wind-up toy. It is as large as a duck and it associates with ducks in open water, yet the Coot is a Rail rather than a Duck. The "Mudhen," as it is sometimes called, is a dark, *slate gray bird with a whitish chicken-like bill.* The base of the bill extends far enough up the forehead to be noticeably different from duck bills. It is quite white as well, contrasting with the dark plumage, and *it is this bird's surest identification mark.*

Most of the Coot's life is spent on the water, usually on ponds where grass and reeds grow. It propels itself along through the water using feet which are lobed along both sides of its separate toes; it does not have the sort of fully webbed feet that ducks have. These feet aid in its "running on water" habit, the long running take-off, with feet skittering and wingtips beating, which the Coot needs to lift its heavy body into the air.

When swimming, the Coot gives the impression its feet are somehow attached directly to its head because of the characteristic bobbing or pecking motions it makes with each stroke as it glides over the surface of the pond.

During migration, ducks seem to welcome the company of Coots, for marsh ducks frequently flock with it. But Coots, unlike ducks, are not much sport as targets, and most hunters avoid them. That's a good thing for the Coot because this comic fellow is relatively tame. Coots are omnivorous eaters which consume anything edible—plant or animal—that explorations of the pond water and bottom chance to produce.

All of our state is home to the Coot during the warm months when a nest of vegetable trash from the pond bottom is built on supports of marsh plants growing out of the water. The hen lays from 8 to 16 eggs over a period of several days, eggs which are grayish white and finely speckled with black, brown and gray. As incubation begins with the first egg, the nest becomes a scene of eggs intact, young hatching, and youngsters emerging all at one time over a period of days. Each newly hatched chick, clothed in black down except for a bright orange head and bald pate, soon tumbles out of the nest into the water where a waiting parent takes charge and cares for it.

The Coot is found throughout the Great Lakes region during the summer, the majority of them in the southern half of the Lower Peninsula. They migrate to our southern states and as far as Ecuador during the winter.

Key Natural History References: Fredrickson 1977, Stewart and Kantrud 1972, Bent 1926, Fredrickson 1970, Gullion 1953.

Coot

13-16 inches

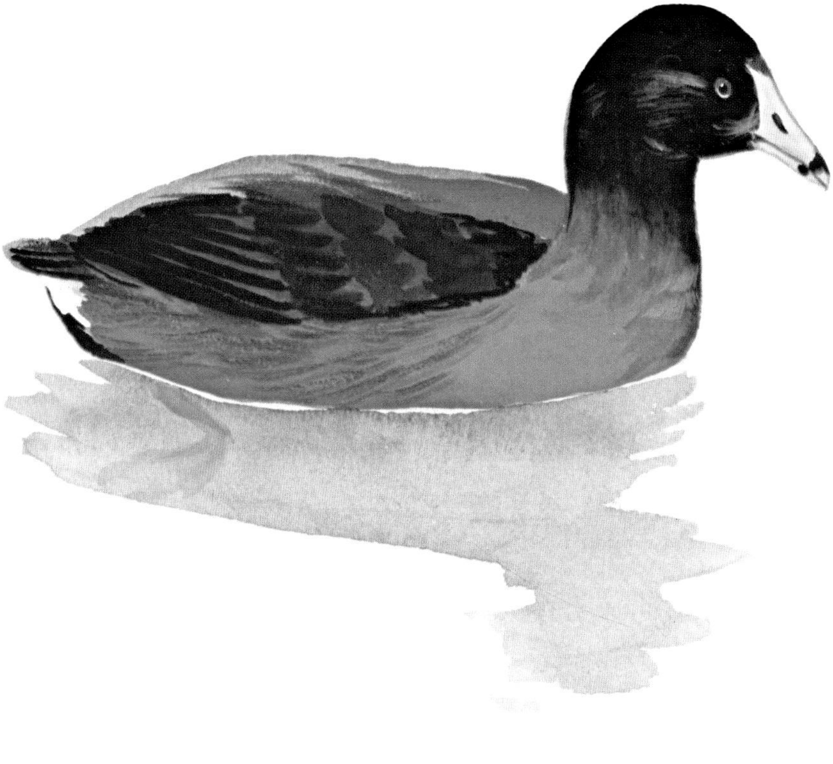

Common Tern *Sterna hirundo*

The Common Tern, which is in fact Michigan's most common tern, is a pigeon-sized bird, slim and streamlined with a deeply forked tail. It is mostly white, tinged with pearl gray. *It wears a black cap, a pair of bright orange feet, and a black-tipped orange bill which combine with the dusky outer wing feathers to provide the best identification marks of this handsome shorebird.* The immature young have a black patch around the nape of their necks but not on their heads. They also have a dark shoulder patch, and their bills are dark. The sexes are similar in their plumage coloration.

This graceful water-loving tern is like a small sleek Gull but *differs noticeably because of its slender, sharply pointed bill.* Long narrow wings carry these birds in a graceful bounding flight similar to that of a swallow. As they fly, they sweep back and forth in erratic turns, with swooping wing strokes, traveling alone or as pairs. They fly with their bills pointed downward as if constantly searching the water below for food. However, before diving headlong into the water to snatch at small fish, their principal diet, they normally hover for a moment. They seldom are seen swimming, prefering instead to land on driftwood or the shore where they patter about gracefully on short legs and small feet.

While the diet of the Common Tern is mainly small fish, crustaceans and flying insects are also taken. Sometimes, several score of these birds can be seen at a time, gathered on a sand spit where they build nests which are little more than depressions in the sand or pebbles, made by hunkering down and turning their bodies until satisfied that the shallow hole is ready to be lined with grasses. Both parents incubate the two or three olive-brown spotted eggs and both defend the nest and young.

In our region, the Common Tern is no longer so common as it once was. The bird winters from Florida southward, and had almost disappeared from American skies early in this century. In those days, the Tern's feathers were considered an essential decoration on women's hats. But the elimination of the plumage trade and full protection given this pretty bird in 1913 allowed its numbers to recover rapidly. However, predation by gulls, which mingle with Terns along our Great Lakes shores, has steadily reduced Tern numbers here in recent years. The Caspian Tern, also a bird of our region, is similar in appearance, but is much larger and more gull-like in its habits.

Key Natural History References: Bent 1963, Payne 1983.

Green-winged Teal *Anas crecca*

The Green-winged Teal is the more colorful of our region's two species of teal, although it is less frequently seen in the state, especially during summer months. The male Greenwing is *an over-all gray duck of small size with a cinnamon-brown head that has a glossy green patch on either side. However, its most dependable identification mark is a vertical white stripe on its body just ahead of the wings.* Buffy-yellow tail coverts show in any light, but the green head patch is difficult to see in shadows and on gray days. *So watch for a tiny fast-flying duck with a vertical white body stripe ahead of the wings.*

The female Greenwing is speckled brown and has dark wings with a green patch visible both at rest and in flight.

Similar in flight speed to the Bluewing, the Greenwing flies long distances over land in tight little flocks searching for food. They are little winged bullets, moving north in spring, south in fall. Their movements are precise and quick as the flocks twist, turn, and bank in tight formation. On the ground it is especially graceful for a duck.

A hardy little bird, the Greenwing is one of the first arrivals in spring from its southern U.S. winter range. It moves steadily northward as ice melts and rivers and bays open. It comes north well ahead of warm weather, driving on to its breeding grounds in Canada while the weather is still nippy. This teal seldom nests in our state.

All teal forage in shallow water for their food, tipping their heads downward to feed off the bottom. The diets of the Greenwing and the Bluewing are similar in that they both include the seeds of pond-growing plants. While teal often feed in inter-mixed flocks, the Greenwing consumes more seeds, but less animal and other vegetable matter than the Bluewing. Snails, however, are eaten steadily where found. And they will also visit grainfields, being quite at home on land as well as water.

The Greenwing male's call is a high-pitched staccato whistle, but there is a softer call which can be confused with the song of spring peepers. The female utters a faint descending *"quack,"* her only contribution to the conversation. The Bluewing is a somewhat quieter bird, the male lisping a high-pitched, but soft *"tseeeel"* usually when in flight. Its mate's call is a more duck-like *"quack"* but still weak compared to that of a Mallard, for example.

The whistling wings and mellow lisping notes of the teal signal the arrival in spring of two of our state's most pleasing water birds. Their presence during spring migration, mixed in with flocks of larger ducks and coots, is a diminutive treat for all birdwatchers, and especially those who love to tramp around marshlands in the early spring chill.

Key Natural History References: Bellrose 1976, Palmer 1976 v.2, Johnsgard 1975.

Female

Male

Barn Owl *Tyto alba*

The Barn Owl is a bird worth the effort of the search, although it is no longer common in our region, partly it seems because its favored habitat, lofty barn interiors, are no longer so commonly available. Also, because of its nocturnal habits, it is seldom seen in daylight, so it may live in many neighborhoods without anyone recording its presence. In fact, the Barn Owl is one of the most ghostly of birds. It appears to be all white when seen from below as it flies noiseless as a huge moth through the night. As if to add to its supernatural aura, the Barn Owl does not hoot, but utters long screams and unbirdlike hisses. It often lives in deserted barns, church steeples, belfries and, of course, *haunted houses*, a favorite owl roost!

A grown Barn Owl is Crow size and has *a heart-shaped ruff of feathers around a monkey-like face. Its back is tawny or buff colored and is speckled with brown; the face and underparts are a creamy white. It has dark eyes and no ear tufts. Absurdly long legs are also distinguishing*. For its body size the Barn Owl has a wide wingspan often reaching nearly four feet.

A night stalker, this excellent hunter searches farmlands and marshes for mice, ground squirrels, and similar small ground mammals which it eats in prodigious quantities. The Barn Owl seems always hungry and can eat its own weight in a single night. As with other owls, it eats its prey by gulping it down, flesh, bones, fur and all. What it doesn't digest is regurgitated as solid little pellets in the manner of most owls. Lacking teeth, their digestive systems do the work of removing flesh from bones and fur. When perched, this owl commonly lowers its head and swings it back and forth, creating a grotesque appearance as it pivots to and fro on its long legs.

Tolerant of civilization, this owl is sometimes an unnoticed resident of towns and even cities. It chooses a variety of places to nest, including empty buildings. It will also take over the deserted nest cavity of another bird and at times will even lay its five to seven eggs on the ground.

The female will begin incubating the first egg as soon as it's laid, so that the nest will eventually be full of young of various sizes, all with the common traits of snapping bills, hissing cries, and a general unfriendliness. When hunting is not so productive, the largest and strongest of the young gets the food, causing the smaller young to starve. The loss of nestlings in this way contributes to the general scarcity of this bird in our region, and though still numerous elsewhere, this bird's numbers have dwindled sharply in recent years in our region, with only a few nesting pairs reported.

The wide-ranging Barn Owl is at home from southern Canada south through Central America. They also live in Eurasia, Africa, the Orient and Australia. They remain year-round residents where found in our Great Lakes region.

Key Natural History References: Wallace 1948, Bent 1938, Stewart 1952, Payne 1983.

94

Barn Owl   14-20 inches

Cooper's Hawk *Accipiter cooperii*
Sharp-shinned Hawk *Accipiter striatus*

The Cooper's and Sharp-shinned Hawks are almost photocopies of each other, though the Sharpshin looks as if it's a miniature of the Cooper's. Yet, since for both birds the sexes are similar in coloration, with females being a bit larger than males, it is nearly impossible to distinguish a large female Sharpshin from a male Cooper's Hawk. Both species are *Accipiters*: that is, they are *long-tailed, streamlined hawks with rather short rounded wings and small heads.* They are direct fliers, alternating groups of a few wing-beats with glides. Seldom are they very high in the sky, for they are not soaring birds.

The Cooper's Hawk is about the size of a crow, while the body of a Sharpshin is not much larger than that of a Robin. The Cooper's wingspread is two and a half to nearly three feet; the Sharpshin's is a little less than two feet. Both have blue-gray backs and rusty colored underparts. Their most apparent distinguishing features are the tips of their tails, and this is most obvious only when the birds are at rest with tails folded. *The Cooper's Hawk has a rounded tail, the Sharpshin a square or slightly notched tail.*

Their habits are similar and their food varies only to the extent of its size and each hawk's ability to catch it. Both are restless, dashing hunters. The Cooper's is especially fast and powerful. In years past it earned the nickname Chicken Hawk because of its lightning raids on hen yards and fast departures with startled farmers' pullets. However, the "Chicken Hawk" continues to survive in our region, living mostly on mammals as it always has, seeming to show a preference for ground squirrels. Cooper's Hawks are large enough and strong enough to carry off a grown rabbit or grouse should one appear, but the Sharpshin's primary diet is small birds, up to pigeon size. Whatever the prey, both Cooper's and Sharpshins use surprise and great speed to make their attacks successful.

Both hawks nest in trees, usually high above the ground, building their own or using abandoned nests of other hawks, usually roughly built affairs of sticks and twigs. The Cooper's frequently uses the same nest for several years, making additions and repairs each year as necessary.

These two strikingly handsome hawks have reputations far worse than they deserve—if a bird's worth has to be measured in its benefits to humans. And we can rejoice now, because through protection their numbers appear to be increasing slowly.

Both the Cooper's and the Sharpshin are year-round residents of the southern Great Lakes region and both are also found throughout our northern states and into Canada during summer months.

Key Natural History References, Coopers Hawk: Bent 1937, Craighead and Craighead 1969, Forbush 1929. Key Natural History References, Sharpshin: Platt 1976, Bent 1937, Mendall 1944, Craighead and Craighead 1969.

Cooper's Hawk   (right)   14-20 inches
Sharp-shinned Hawk   (left)

Blue-winged Teal *Anas discors*

There are two Michigan species of teal, those small sleek ducks which look so tiny when flocking with other larger ducks. Teal are about half the size of Mallards and fly their erratic courses in compact little flocks.

The most commonly seen here is the Blue-winged Teal, a dainty, colorful little duck of Great Lakes region marshes, grassy ponds and slow-flowing streams.

The male Bluewing is a dull, mottled brown color with a pinkish cast overall. *It is best identified by the white crescent just in front of its eyes, by its small size, and by the large blue wing patch which produces its name.* There is also a white patch on its flanks, and the tail is black. However, the male molts into eclipse plumage in July and August and so, for the rest of the year, resembles the female which generally is mottled brown but with the same distinctive blue wing patch as the male.

Blue-winged Teal fly swiftly. They give the impression of moving at blistering speeds which early observers guessed at 100 miles an hour. However, more accurate modern clocking has put the speed at a much more conservative 30 to 40 miles an hour. Because of their small size and rapid wingbeat, they just seem to be going much faster. As do most dabblers, Bluewings spring straight up from the water, as if driven by springs, and are off downwind as soon as they take off. When landing, a flock will pass, then repass over the landing spot before they feel certain it is safe enough to plop abruptly into the water.

The Bluewing nests in grassy sites in meadows and hayfields often at some distance from water, although occasionally it will use as a nesting site the top of a muskrat house, or a sedge tussock surrounded by water.

Bluewings arrive on their Great Lakes region nesting grounds in May, and despite their small size, they are very prolific, a nest typically holding 8 to 11 eggs, and sometimes as many as 15. Incubation lasts about 24 days, but once the young are out of the shell, they dry off and immediately head for the water. During nesting, the female does the sitting; her mate will defend her against intruders, rather than try to control a large uncertain area. Some begin a gradual southward movement as early as August, although they are frequently seen in the region as late as November. Some winter in the southern U.S., but the majority of Bluewings continue on south in the fall as far as South America where they remain until late spring. Consequently, the migratory travels of some of these little birds are impressive. One taken in Ecuador had been banded in Manitoba 4000 miles away, and another had flown 7000 miles from Saskatchewan to meet its fate in a Peruvian marsh.

Key Natural History References: Bennett 1938, Palmer 1976 v.2, Bellrose 1976, Johnsgard 1975.

Male

Female

Spruce Grouse *Canachites canadensis*

The Spruce Grouse can be a startling bird, not because of explosive departures from nearby undergrowth, such as its cousin the Ruffed Grouse is famous for, but for just the opposite reason. The Spruce Grouse stays put and sits tight, often perching on the lower limb of a spruce a few feet away or just ahead of you, all the while cocking a curious eye at you. It seems to be completely unafraid, almost stupidly so, which is why hunters and woodsworkers have given it the colorful name "Fool Hen."

The Spruce Grouse is the size of a small chicken, 15 to 17 inches in body length. *The male has striking markings which make it easy to identify when seen here,* generally in the northern third of our Great Lakes region where it lives year-round. *It is slate gray above with a black belly, breast, and chin. Its sides are spotted with white and the undersides are a splotchy black and white. In the male there is a spot of bare red skin about the eyes and a chestnut, almost red, band of color extends across the end of the broad dark tail. The female is a more mottled brown or rust color over-all, barred alternately with darker brown.* It is somewhat darker than the hen Ruffed Grouse, and lacks the male's black on face, chest, and belly; it is perfectly camouflaged, however, when among dry leaves in our northern forest.

The Spruce Grouse lives in spruce woods and tamarack swamps where it is still fairly common in our northern woodlands. However, its numbers appear to thin out locally when civilization or too much human activity takes over its old haunts. In short, though it appears slow to learn, it soon grows wary if bothered too frequently.

Its flesh is not particularly tasty, and consequently it is not a favored game bird with hunters. A quiet bird, this grouse's main call is a low-pitched hooting. In summer the diet is made up of insects, berries, tender leaves, and mushrooms which it gathers by scratching and pecking. In winter, spruce and tamarack buds are its principal food.

In May or June, the hen lays eight to fifteen brown speckled eggs in a nest usually well concealed on the ground under low conifer branches or in brush heaps. The young leave the nest with the hen as soon as they have dried off and fluffed up—usually only a few hours after hatching. They begin their search for food immediately, with the protective hen as their teacher. During courtship, the male shows off while in flight and struts on the ground to attract the hen. These birds are year-round residents of our northern regions, and as is typical with most grouse, probably live out their lives in a fairly small area. In extreme cold weather they move deeper into dense forests for protection and stick to less windy lowlands until the warmer months arrive.

Key Natural History References: Ellison 1971 and 1973, Fritz 1977, Bent 1932, Forbush and May 1939.

Female

Male

Ring-necked Duck *Aythya collaris*

The Ring-necked Duck is a black and white diving duck which is often found in heavily wooded areas. It stays in flooded swamps and marshes where there is abundant sedge, and in beaver flowages near large wooded lakes and rivers. Expanses of open water are necessary so it can trip along the surface while getting airborne.

The neck band between breast and neck which gives this duck its name is indistinct and not nearly so noticeable as the *two white bands across its blue bill—one at the base, the other near the tip.* Hunters, consequently, prefer to call it a Ringbill.

The male has a black head and a chalky-white crescent between its black chest and gray sides. His black head appears to be slightly crested and is high-domed with a purple gloss which can be noted at close range and in good light. The neck is dark red.

A good field mark of the male when sitting in the water is the white band on the side of the breast just ahead of the folded wing. It appears to be a bar but is actually a continuation of the white under the wing, revealed when the wing is spread.

The female is dark brown, darkest at the crown of the head and on the back and pale brown at the base of the bill. *She can be recognized by a white eye-ring and a prominent white band of feathers around the bill.*

Both sexes show a broad gray wing stripe in flight.

Eighty per cent of the Ringneck's diet is plant food which includes seeds, root stocks, tubers, and stems and leaves of underwater plants taken on dives to the bottom. It prefers water up to five feet deep but is capable of going as deep as 40 feet, and can stay submerged up to a minute. When diving, it keeps its wings folded tightly to its sides and depends on its powerful legs and feet to propel itself downward.

Ringed-necks are seen in Michigan most often during migration for they continue on north to nest in Canada. They return southward from mid-September into late November. Winters are spent from the central U.S. to as far south as the Gulf of Mexico.

The Ringneck is not one of Michigan's most common ducks, but the male's weak, wheezy whistle and his mate's harsh "*cherr*" can be heard spring and fall on most Michigan marshes. As soon as the ponds are clear of ice in spring this duck appears in small flocks along the edges of marshy ponds and sloughs.

Key Natural History References: Mendall 1958, Bellrose 1976, Palmer 1976 v.3, Johnsgard 1975.

Female

Male

Lesser Scaup *Aythya affinis*
Greater Scaup *Aythya marila*

The Greater and Lesser Scaup are black and white ducks with blue bills and marked similarities.

The Scaup Ducks, together, are commonly known as Bluebills. They are so similar that even experienced birdwatchers have difficulty telling one from the other. In both species the male is white with a dark, almost black head, neck, chest and tail, and fine gray markings on the lighter parts of the body. There is sometimes a greenish cast to the head of the male Greater Scaup, and a purple cast to that of the Lesser. But these are faint differences at best, normally only seen with the bird in hand. In both species, the female is brown and has a broad white band on her face around the bill. In flight all show a *broad white stripe* near the rear of their wings. On the water, the males of both species are *dark on both ends, white in the middle and, as noted, the bills are a pale blue.*

The Greater Scaup has a longer wing stripe and rounder head than the Lesser, and the Lesser is more plentiful in our region. The Lesser, which is more often found inland, also has a smaller fingernail-like projection, or pick, at the tip of its bill than that of the Greater. Again, this can only be used to distinguish when the birds are in hand. Seen together, some of these markings are more obvious; seen alone, however, your identification is almost sure to be less certain.

Scaup are usually seen in sizeable bunches, ranging from a few loosely assembled units to rafts of thousands. They prefer the open water of the Great Lakes, also bays and harbors where they shift about in short flights as they move from one feeding ground to another. When alarmed, they require a lengthy expanse of open water for a long running take-off. In migration they travel in large, fast-moving bunches.

Both species are divers and are capable of staying under water for up to a minute. They prefer water less than twenty feet deep where both species seek a diet of aquatic seeds, plants, insects and mollusks. They are truly omniverous, seeking a mixed diet of plant and animal foods, and frequently feeding heavily on any single available item.

These ducks are seen in Michigan most often during migration, for they continue on north to nest, the Greater to Hudson's Bay and beyond, the Lesser to the prairies of Manitoba, Saskatchewan and beyond. They arrive in our Great Lakes region from the south as soon as the waters are open, coming from their winter range in our southern states and along our East and Gulf Coasts. Some Lesser Scaup winter on ocean bays as far north as Boston, while some Greater Scaup will winter north to the Maritime Provinces of eastern Canada.

Key Natural History References: Johnsgard 1975, Palmer 1976 v.3, Bellrose 1976.

Lesser Scaup   15-18 inches
Greater Scaup   16-20 inches

Greater
Male

Female

Male

Ruffed Grouse *Bonasa umbellus*

The Ruffed Grouse is a woodland bird full of surprises. Often the first hint of its presence is when it explodes into the air with a rush of wings, nimbly dodging saplings and tree limbs. In seconds the bird is gone and all is silent again. Take another step, and there may be another feathered explosion at your feet, as its partner makes its dash to new cover.

The Ruffed Grouse springs into the air in this fashion without warning, unless the watcher is alert enough to hear its gentle clucking. Also called Partridge, or "Pat" by hunters, this leaf-colored chicken-like bird is about the size of a pullet, or large bantam. Its *mottled red or brown coloration with its ruff of dark feathers around the neck* makes it almost invisible against the forest floor. *Its large fan-shaped tail,* which is spread in flight, is its surest identifying mark.

When in grouse country, which includes most brushy areas of the northern Great Lakes states, the watcher soon understands why the Ruffed Grouse has been called the "King of Game Birds." And even though thousands of hunters answer its challenge every fall, it is so prolific and resourceful that hunting seems not to affect its numbers from year to year. Rather, its numbers each fall reflect the type of nesting season, the amount of habitat, and the weather patterns that prevailed that spring and summer. Grouse are as numerous today as they were 30 years ago, perhaps even more so.

The drumming of the Ruffed Grouse fills the woodland with sound each spring, and the same sound can be heard throughout the summer and fall. Drumming is done by the male, from an elevation—a log or stump—where he stands erect and beats the air with his wings. As the wings beat faster and faster the bup-bup-bup-up-up-up-br-brr-r-r-r sound increases in speed and volume before dying away slowly. On a still day it can be heard for half a mile, yet listeners often are not sure if they are feeling, rather than hearing, pulses of sound within their own ears. These muffled drumbeats serve as a spring mating call, as well as a false call—or practice—in the fall.

The male is polygamous, so the female tends to the nesting and brooding alone. Eight to twelve whitish eggs are laid in a simple dry leaf nest on the ground. The hen's plumage hides the nest perfectly, and when she leaves briefly to feed, she spreads leaves over the eggs. As soon as the downy young are dry, the family abandons the nest and the daily search for food begins.

Food consists of wild berries and other fruit, grain and weed seeds, tender sapling buds, and acorns and nuts. In winter, when the grouse seeks the cover of conifers, the diet consists mainly of buds. For protection in winter, a Ruffed Grouse will sometimes plummet headlong into a snowbank, then burrow deeper and spend the night out of sight, safe from owls and foxes.

Key Natural History References: Bent 1932, Svoboda and Gullion 1972, Bump et al. 1947, Gullion 1972.

red phase

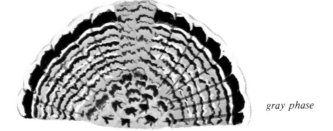

gray phase

Pileated Woodpecker *Dryocopus pileatus*

The Pileated Woodpecker always surprises the birdwatcher with its appearance. *As large and black as a Crow, but with white underwings, a stunning bright red crest, and a raucous call*, it makes a whole forest pause to watch.

Even the work of this giant woodpecker is spectacular. Not one to peck daintily at tree bark, the Pileated whacks and hammers and chisels deep into the interiors of dead trees, spraying huge chips in all directions and producing deep vertical cavities that mark the trail of the bird's hunt for burrowing insects and grubs. The sound is loud and has been described as a drum roll. It is sharply heavier in volume than what other woodpeckers make, and can normally be heard substantial distances.

Its local and colloquial names give an idea of its character: "Cock of the Woods," "Lord God Woodpecker," "Log Cock," and, strangely, "Wood Cock."

As it flies from tree to tree it literally bellows its loud *"cock, cock, cock"* call as if to call attention to itself—just in case the observer had been unable to see its large size, bright plumage and distinctive undulating flight.

There can be no mistaking this bird once seen, and you'll realize immediately that it's indeed a Pileated Woodpecker. *Its large size, woodpecker habits, and long neck capped with that bright red crest all lead to that conclusion.* While it ranges widely for food, it does not migrate and appears to live its life, summer and winter, in the same forest area.

At one time, when this region was more heavily forested, the Pileated was common in all parts of the state. Now its sparse population is mainly located in the Upper Peninsula, although there are a few counties in the Lower Peninsula with significant numbers also. As forests of second growth trees continue to mature throughout our region, the Pileated appears to be increasing its numbers slowly.

The Pileated nests in deep holes it chops out of tree trunks, high up in dead trees. There the female lays three to six white eggs which the male and female alternately incubate until the brood hatches. There is some evidence that Pileated Woodpeckers mate for life after a sort of courtship dance in which both birds take part. Incidentally, *the female can be distinguished from the male because she lacks a red cheek patch beneath her eye, very obvious on the male.*

After the young are raised, the abandoned nest holes often become homes to other burrow dwellers such as Screech Owls, Kestrels, and Wood Ducks.

Like the Loon and the Raven, the Pileated Woodpecker has come to symbolize the deep forests of our northern region, where, when infrequently seen, it brings unique excitement to a day's hunt or hike.

Key Natural History References: Bent 1939, Conner et al. 1975, Graber et al. 1977, Hoyt 1957, Bull 1975.

Green Heron *Butorides striatus*

Observers of this common Michigan wading bird have a difficult time seeing the green coloration because the Green Heron, even at a short distance, looks almost black and is much more dark blue than green in its body plumage. *It is a small heron, smaller than a crow, has short legs, a chestnut-colored neck and dark crest which it elevates when alarmed. Its yellowish or orange legs are distinctive.*

The Green Heron gives the impression that it is either tame or stupid, though neither is probably the case, because it seems able to distinguish readily between its friends and enemies. When nervous, it twitches its tail up and down and raises and lowers its crest. When threatened, it freezes in place, attempting to hide by immobility. Young birds at the nest soon learn this defense. When Green Herons fly off in alarm crying their loud "*Skeow,*" they typically drop a long white 'chalk line' on the water. *In flight this stocky bird, with head folded back on its S-shaped neck, looks like a crow. The flight is rapid with deep down strokes.*

The Green Heron is the most common of all Great Lakes region herons. It is found haunting the edges of ponds, lakes, rivers, marshes and even wet meadows. Paddle up a sluggish stream and the chances are good that a "Fly Up the Creek" will emerge ahead of your boat in direct, swift flight, calling your boat a "skeow" as it flies, then landing in the branches of an overhanging tree where it will perch and watch in statue-still silence until frightened off again.

In addition to the "Skeow" call, which is similar to the sound made by blowing over a blade of grass held taut between a person's thumbs, there is also a bullfrog-like call and one which sounds like a young crow. The Green Heron's vocabulary has no melodies, but it's as much a part of the lowlands as the cattails themselves.

A variety of small fish, crustaceans, mollusks, insects, reptiles, amphibians, spiders and leeches are victims of the Green Heron's hunting methods, which are a combination of quiet wading and slow stalking through shallow water and wet vegetation. While some individuals defend separate feeding territories, many Green Herons will share a common feeding ground.

The bird's nest, which is a careless collection of twigs, may be found close to water or at some distance away in evergreen trees or orchards. Usually it is from 10 to 15 feet above ground, but occasionally the nest is on a ground hummock in a favorite marsh. Four or five blue eggs are the usual clutch. Green Herons are both solitary and colonial in nesting. While most often the nest is found alone, occasionally as many as 30 pairs will nest in close proximity to each other. A summer bird here, this heron spends its winters in the southern United States.

Key Natural History References: Palmer 1962, Kushlan 1976, Bent 1926.

Green Heron   16-22 inches

Wood Duck *Aix sponsa*

At the turn of the century the Wood Duck was a rare bird in the Great Lakes region, but enlightened conservation and stringent controls on hunting have returned it to former numbers. Today it is as plentiful as it was in the mid 19th Century. Great Lakes region birdwatchers rejoice in this recovery, for many see the Wood Duck as our most beautiful duck. It is indeed a resplendently colored bird.

The male in its spring breeding plumage and in fall and winter is so bright and varied it is almost a shocking sight on a quiet pond or on the limbs of a tree. Bright, delicate and graceful, it is difficult to describe without an excess of superlatives. Even its Latin species name means "bride."

No other duck has the long slicked-back crest of the Wood Duck. In flight, *good field marks are a large head, short neck, long square tail, and dark breast and wings. In spring, the male's head is darkly iridescent, eyes orange, head streaked with white, and the bill a varied pattern of red, yellow, white and black. Four colors on the bill alone! The back is dark and iridescent, the breast a rich burgundy, the belly white and the wings dark.* The female is much duller, but still striking. Her head has the crest but it's grayish; *she has a prominent white teardrop-shaped eye-ring around dark eyes. Her bill is black, her throat white and her back, breast and flanks are brown in differing shades.*

During the summer the male slides into eclipse plumage and resembles the female. However, he maintains the bright bill and lacks the white eye-ring. His underparts are white.

As its name implies, the Wood Duck prefers streams and ponds surrounded by woods, or with woods nearby. When alarmed it often flies swiftly into woods where it adeptly dodges trees and limbs and soon disappears. It often roosts and rests on tree limbs far above the ground.

At nesting time the female finds a tree cavity or uses a nesting box from three to fifty feet above ground. Here she will lay 12 to 14 eggs, and occasionally other Wood Duck hens will add their eggs as well, producing an enormous brood. When the young are hatched and still in down, the female coaxes them to the nest hole opening from which they tumble to the ground below and follow her to nearby water. Being lightweight and fluffy, they are seldom injured by such a fall. Wood Ducks are largely vegetarian, fattening in fall on acorns, but varying their diet with grasshoppers.

The male's call is a high-pitched and unducklike sound described as an ascending *"jeeeeeeee"* or *"peet-peet."* Its alarm call is a *"hoo-eek, hoo-eek"* although the latter is more often attributed to the female. The Wood Duck's winter range includes our southern states, south to the Caribbean islands.

Key Natural History References:
Palmer 1976 v.3, Bellrose 1976,
Hester and Dermid 1973, Grice and
Rogers 1965, Coulter 1957.

Female

Male

American Crow *Corvus brachyrhynchos*
Northern Raven *Corvus corax*

The common or American Crow and the Raven are this region's two big black birds; and in spite of the fact that there is a recognizable difference in size, the two are often confused when seen at a distance.

The raucous, mischievous Crow is one of the state's best known birds. It is noted for its intelligence and for both its tolerance and suspicion of humans; for its colorful behavior and its occasional destructiveness.

The Raven, a bird of the northern Great Lakes region, whose reputation is already established in the mind of anyone who's read Poe's "The Raven," is more shy, impressive and dignified.

The Crow measures about 20 inches in body length while the Raven is up to six inches larger. The Raven's large bill is higher, in profile, than it is broad. The Raven has a shaggy-appearing throat, caused by distinctive pointed feathers, and its tail is wedge-shaped. However, these identifying marks are little help when the birds are far away—as they usually are. The difference in flight is probably the best clue to identification. *The Crow flies with steady wing flaps while the Raven alternately flaps a bit and then soars, sailing along on stiffly-extended horizontal wings.*

The Crow is both damned and loved. It is a clever bird with a passion for stealing and hiding anything it can, especially bright-colored objects.

In the wild, the Crow is so cautiously alert it is difficult to surprise. When in a flock, there seems always to be one bird on watch, and its cries of alarm alert the others to any approaching intruder. Hunters are convinced the wily bird knows the difference between an unarmed human and one carrying a gun. That may be carrying things a bit far, but there's no doubt of the Crow's alertness and keen eyesight.

The Raven prefers deep, secluded woods and it too is a wary bird. Unlike the Crow, whose "*Caw, Caw, Caw*" is well known, the Raven has a varied vocabulary of coarse croaks, grunts and screams. Its clucking has a metallic sound and sometimes reminds one of an old farm pump being primed.

Both birds have a varied diet, depending upon the season. Crows eat mice, crayfish, snails and such insect life as grasshoppers, beetles, and caterpillars. They have an appetite for earth-softened seed corn which make them the inspiration for scarecrows and rifle targets for angry farmers. Both birds feed on carrion. The Raven, probably because it avoids farmland, does no damage to crops and seldom irritates human neighbors.

Both the Crow and the Raven are year-round residents of our region. Although they are usually found farther north, a few Ravens are beginning to appear in some Lower Peninsula counties, especially in winter.

Key Natural History References, Crow: Bent 1946, Goodwin 1976, Johnston 1961, Payne 1983. Raven: Bent 1946, Goodwin 1976, Hooper 1977, Harlow 1922, J.J. Murray, 1940, Tyrrell 1945, Payne 1983.

Crow   17-21 inches

Raven   22-27 inches

Raven

Crow

Barred Owl *Strix varia*

This large gray owl, the "Eight Hooter," is the night voice of the deep woods. In eight equally accented hoots it seems to ask, "*Who cooks for you? Who cooks for you all?*" The call is in two groups of four, a "hoohoo-hoohoo … hoohoo-hoohoo-ow" dropping in volume and accent at the end. The end note isn't strong enough to be considered a full hoot, so it isn't really a "Nine Hooter."

As do most owls, this big predator hunts largely at night, but it is often seen in daylight as well, for it has good daytime vision. *Its distinctive horizontal barring on the breast, abruptly joined by vertical streaks on the belly, plus its dark eyes and round puffy head mark it as the Barred Owl.* It generally presents a view of being an over-all gray brown with a liberal spotting of white on its back. Among woodland birds it is a mild-mannered giant measuring from 18 to 22 inches in body length, and is less fierce and not so large as the Great Horned Owl, whose habitat it shares over most of North America, including the entire Great Lakes region, where it is a year-round resident.

In deep dark woods it hunts on noiseless wings moving on light, buoyant flights at twilight and throughout the night. The easy slow wingbeats especially mark its silent progress, as it hunts for food which is easiest to find—mice, frogs, reptiles, crayfish, spiders, and some small birds.

If you are fortunate enough to observe the Barred Owl during courtship, you'll hear a good deal of loud hooting, much like wild laughter, and a variety of similarly urgent love notes, moving down the range all the way to a soft cooing sound. You will also see both male and female nod and bow with half-opened wings, wobbling their bodies and twisting their heads.

The nest is a tree cavity or, when none is available, an abandoned hawk or squirrel nest, commonly located in a large tree, white pines being preferred. The nesting pair return to the same cavity or its vicinity year after year, sometimes for two or three decades. They do little nest building, but their own loose feathers found in an area are a clue that a nest is nearby. In March or April the female lays two or three pure white eggs and the pair then raise their young over much of the summer.

Barred Owls share the same wet or swampy woodland with the Red-Shouldered Hawk and there are even records of the two species using the same nest at different times in a single year. As is true with most Michigan owls, the Barred Owl's worst enemy is a flock of Crows or Jays. A continuous raucous gathering of these birds heard in a woodland can mean that there is a sleepy, harassed owl in their midst. But a nightime visit by the owl to a roosting site can mean there is one less Crow or Jay, too. The Barred Owl is a year-round resident of our state.

Key Natural History References: Bent 1938, Forbush 1929, Errington and McDonald 1937.

Northern Harrier *Circus cyaneus*

The male and female Northern Harrier look as if they are different species. Each is striking, and an exciting spectacle, in its own right. The male is the large gray hawk *with a large white rump patch*; the female is the brown hawk with *the same white patch at the base of its tail*. The male's underparts are white; the female's brownish white. *Both are slim birds with long rounded wings and long tails.* Each has an imperfect facial ruff which gives it a slightly owlish appearance. The male is the whitest of our Great Lakes Hawks and has a further distinguishing mark of black wingtips. As if these color differences were not enough, the immature Northern Harrier has a rich russet chest and belly.

Also known as the Marsh Hawk, the Northern Harrier prefers as habitat low open fields and marshes. You will identify it as a large hawk—about 18 inches in body length with a wingspan of more than three feet—which flies systematically back and forth only a few feet above the ground as it hunts. As it flies the wings tend to slant upward and the bird tips from side to side. It flies lightly and gracefully in long sweeps searching the marsh or field below as it hunts. Often it hunts in pairs and, when the young are still with their parents, the whole family hunts together. When prey is sighted, the Harrier brakes in flight and plummets toward it, talons outstretched. The diet consists mainly of small mammals, birds, mice, and other marsh creatures.

Unlike most other hawks, the Northern Harrier rests and roosts on the ground, or on low perches such as fence posts, rather than in trees. It seldom soars, being most at home close to the ground. However, during spring courtship, males fly much higher and make grand dangerous-looking dives, ending near ground with sharp upturns and stalls, followed by more dives. Sometimes several will be seen together performing in this way and, in migration, this bird will fly high and soar as it goes.

The nest is built on the ground, in deep grass, and is composed of selected finely dried marsh grasses. There the female lays four to six greenish or bluish white eggs marked with light brown spots. Both parents incubate the eggs and both are fierce defenders of the nest. They will not hesitate to fly at human intruders, talons extended, making binoculars and distance the safest way to make this bird's acquaintance. Still, in habit and appearance, the Harrier seems to be one of the gentler hawks. It is much at home with its environment. Its reputation as a good mouse-catcher is deserved. Its traditional name adds a note of ancient romance to this truly grand bird. Unfortunately, in our region this bird has decreased greatly in numbers since 1960, although in parts of the Upper Peninsula and the northern Lower Peninsula the Harrier population has held steady in recent years.

Cold weather sends it southward to most of our southern states, and as far south as the Bahamas, Cuba, and Columbia in South America.

Key Natural History References: Bent 1937, Hausman 1966, Randall 1940, Hecht 1951.

17½-24 inches

Female

Male

Redhead *Aythya americana*
Canvasback *Aythya valisineria*

The Canvasback and Redhead Ducks are similar enough in appearance to cause some minor confusion in their identification. Both are roughly Mallard size, both have reddish heads, dark breasts and light colored backs, but there are enough distinctions so that identifying one from another is not a major problem. The confusion here is slight when compared to that we find trying to identify some of the warblers, for example.

The Canvasback is the larger and has a noticeably lighter back. Its flatheaded profile with *long sloping forehead* in a continuous line to the tip of the bill is an easy field mark and makes it an especially handsome bird, favored by both hunters and watchers. In flight, it is a white looking front-heavy bird whose pale gray back and white sides are delicately lined in a wave-like pattern which suggests the surface appearance of canvas fabric, from which it gets its name. The male's head and neck are rust red and his black breast extends to the waterline. The female "Can" has the reddish head and neck, but over-all is more grayish.

The Redhead, on the other hand, has a *large round head*, the male's red, the female's gray. The female has an indistinct face patch near the bill and over-all is a much grayer bird than her mate. Both have a blue bill that has a black hooked tip. Both lack the white appearance of the Canvasback.

The Canvasback is agile and graceful in the water, but needs a long run for take-offs, being so heavy-bodied. It is a very swift flier, and has been clocked at 72 miles per hour. The flocks fly in long strings and in loose V formations. The Canvasback is a favorite game bird and normally has spicy flavored flesh because it feeds so heavily on wild celery, its preferred food.

The Redhead is commonly seen in our region on ponds and lakes, but prefers the deeper waters of Great Lakes bays and shore edges. It is seen here primarily on the eastern side of the state. While not as fast as the Canvasback, it is a rapid flier and it also migrates in long strings or V formations.

The food of both species is similar, with seeds and aquatic plants making the bulk of it. When feeding, the birds dabble and tip up, immersing their heads and necks as geese do. Red-heads, when food is scarce, often continue to feed after dark.

Both these birds winter on lakes and bays in large flocks from the northern United States south to the Gulf of Mexico. In migration they fly at high altitude and at great speed.

Key Natural History References, Canvasback: Hockbaum 1944, Johnsgard 1975, Bellrose 1976. Redhead: Bellrose 1976, Johnsgard 1975, Palmer 1976 v.3, Low 1945.

Redhead (top)   18-23 inches
Canvasback (bottom)   20-24 inches

Male

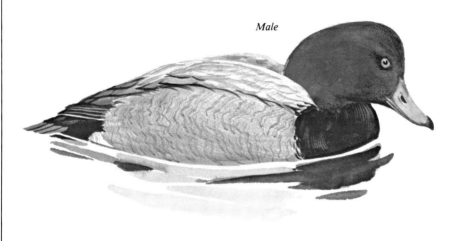

Male

Great Horned Owl *Bubo virginianus*

The Great Horned Owl is a bird which truly commands respect. Having a body nearly two feet long and a 55-inch wingspread, it looks fierce and has a disposition to match. It is abroad at night and its loud hooting call makes dark nights even darker. Known also as the "Hoot Owl" and dubbed "Tiger of the Air," it is Michigan's most impressive owl. The Snowy Owl is as large, and the Great Gray Owl larger, but neither is a full time resident here, and neither is so aggressive, even dangerous at times, to be near.

Its large size, the two-inch tufts of feathers which rise like ears or horns from its head, and its white throat are the best identifying characteristics. The "ears" are especially wide apart and add to the massive appearance of the head. The bird is dark brown with numerous black horizontal bars; its eyes are yellow. Over-all, the Great Horned Owl's stocky body makes it especially powerful looking. And that's no delusion; it is a big, strong, aggressive bird, and the female is noticeably larger than the male.

Because it is primarily but not totally nocturnal, the Great Horned Owl is more often heard than seen. Its characteristic call is a series of three to six or more hoots, typically *"hoo, hoohoo, hoo, hoo,"* or *"hoo, hoo, hoo,"* or *"hoo, hoo, hoohoo."* At certain times of year, especially in spring, two or three of these big birds can make the countryside ring with their calls and answering calls.

Food for this owl is a variety of flesh: partridge, quail, ducks, rabbits, squirrels, rats, and even skunks—which it seems to relish. Crayfish and large insects also are taken. Once damned as a poultry thief, the Great Horned Owl, as with all birds of prey, is now protected in Michigan and most other states. Whatever raids it may have made on hen-yards are infrequent now anyway; most chickens these days live and die inside egg factory buildings and are seldom if ever exposed to the out-of-doors.

The Great Horned Owl chooses a variety of nesting places. Often it is a deserted hawk's nest where the incubating adult looks like a large cat perched on the nest, hence yet another name "Cat Owl." Sometimes the nest is in a tree cavity, sometimes on the ground. Regardless of where it's located, nesting begins very early in the year in our upper Great Lakes region, and frequently there is snow on the ground when the two or three white eggs are laid. In fact, it is frequently still February or early March—before most migrating birds have arrived from the south—when this year-round resident of Michigan begins the cycle of producing and raising its young, a process of hatching, growing and training which will continue until there is frost in the air the following fall.

Key Natural History References: Bent 1938, Forbush 1929, Earhart and Johnson 1970.

Ring-billed Gull *Larus delawarensis*

Many gulls may be seen on or near the waters of our Great Lakes, though only two are truly common in numbers here. Included in the group of visitors, migrants, accidentals, and infrequent residents are the following: The Glaucous, Iceland, Greater Black-backed, Bonaparte's, Sabine's, Franklin, Laughing, and Thayer's Gulls, and the Black-legged Kittiwake. While most viewers will be lucky to see any of these birds, they will almost certainly see the Herring Gull and the Ring-billed Gull, both depicted in this book.

The two gulls are remarkably similar. The Ringbill is four to five inches shorter in body length and has a slightly shorter wingspan than the Herring Gull, but for identification from a distance, this difference will not be much help, even when the two birds are flocked together. The plumage color of the two birds is quite similar and *the only real distinguishing marks are A) a black ring that entirely circles the bill of the Ringbill, and B) a pair of yellowish or greenish legs in the Ringbill, and pinkish legs in the Herring Gull.*

The Ringbill has the same varied vocabulary and vocal sounds that we hear from the Herring Gull—squeals, "rawk-rawk" calls, and a general list of complaints, but in the Ringbill all are softer and higher pitched.

The immature Ringbills are similar in color to the second year Herring Gulls in both their first and second winters, except for being a bit lighter in color and having an inch-wide band of black across the end of the tail. Like the Herring Gulls, young Ringbills do not reach adult plumage until their third year.

The diet of the Ringbill includes fish, carrion found along the shore, and insects, earthworms, and even small rodents when foraging over plowed fields inland. They may be seen in sizable bands during spring and fall plowing, when they wheel and dive and walk behind the plow, picking at whatever is turned up.

Nests are built in colonies with scores and often hundreds of other Ringbills nesting side by side. Usually these are placed near shores on islands or in locations generally undisturbed by humans, dogs, and other animals. Such colonies are often found in company with terns, other gulls, and ducks. The nests themselves are loosely built of shore debris, grass, and weeds, and are commonly placed on open ground or among rocks high up above the level reached by storm waves. Three eggs are a common clutch, and after hatching, the whole scene is one of constant noise and squawks, of Ringbills fluttering up and settling down, of young hatchlings in their gray-brown fluff running about.

Ringbills are seen in our Great Lakes region both winter and summer, though most of their nesting activity is farther north in central Canada, and most winter along our Gulf and Atlantic Coasts.

Key Natural History Reference: Peterson 1980.

Red-tailed Hawk *Buteo jamaicensis*

"**K**ee-r-r-r-r, Kee-er-r-r-r." The shrill scream comes from far above, and against the pale blue background of the summer sky two tiny specks can be seen wheeling in lazy circles far overhead. For hours they circle, riding thermal updrafts apparently for the sheer enjoyment of it all. Earthbound humans can only watch and envy the marvelous flight of this large bird.

The Redtail is the best known of our large hawks here in the Great Lakes region. It is big, heavy-set, and bulky with *wide rounded wings and a broad tail*. The tail, rufous red above and pale pink below, is its most distinguishing mark. From the ground the Redtail is *recognized by its light breast and dark belly band*. In general, the adult is dark brown above, whitish below.

The male's body measures close to two feet in length, the female's a few inches longer. The broad wings spread an impressive four feet from tip to tip. Redtails show considerable color variation from light to dark, however, making identificaton uncertain at times. A thick-bodied hawk that sits erect and quiet in the open on top of a tree is probably a Redtail.

In spite of its also being known as "Hen Hawk," the Redtail feeds largely on mice and small rodents, hunting them in a variety of ways. Even when soaring high in the sky, it may really be hunting, for its eye structure proves it can see a mouse in the open field far below, a sight which may bring it quickly to the ground in a long plunging dive. At other times it hovers motionless in the air near the ground, watching intently. Or it may sit motionless in a treetop surveying the surrounding area for prey. It may be seen so engaged both in the open and in woodlands.

The Redtail appears to move slowly as it hunts, but obviously it is efficient, as anyone who has seen it catching grasshoppers in a mowed field can testify. In the woods, this hawk sometimes hunts in pairs, coordinating efforts to trap squirrels in the open.

The nest is a bulky platform of sticks placed high above the ground in the fork of a tree. Pairs mate for life and may use the same nest for several years. Even though the nests are usually out of harm's reach, the Redtail is more inclined to flight when an intruder approaches than to make any effort to stay with the nest, let alone defend it. The female lays 2 to 4 eggs varying in color from dirty-white or faintly blue to an even pale-green. Incubation lasts about a month, and just one batch of young is raised each year.

Redtails are the most numerous hawks in Michigan's agricultural areas. They are seen throughout the Great Lakes region during the warm months, but those in the northern half drift south a bit in the fall. The winter range of this bird includes the southern half of the Great Lakes region, so you may see them here all year round.

Key Natural History References: Hagar 1957, Gates 1972, Fitch et al. 1946, Craighead and Craighead 1969, Orians and Kuhlman 1956.

Red-breasted Merganser *Mergus serrator*

Red-breasted Mergansers, also known as Sawbills, or Sheldrakes, are fish-catching divers equipped with narrow, pointed bills with saw-like edges that assist them in catching and holding their prey. In body length, this merganser is about 20 to 26 inches long, a bit shorter than the Common Merganser, but larger than the Hooded Merganser. All three are seen here in the Great Lakes region, though mainly in the northern portions during summer months, as we are at the southern edge of their nesting habitat.

All the mergansers are fish eaters, and gather their food by diving in deep water to chase down and consume any small fish they can catch. They vary their diet with crayfish and other aquatic animal life.

The Red-breasted Merganser is one of nature's most striking bits of plumage design. The drake, in spring plumage, has a metallic green headdress, and a waving crest rising off the back of his head. His bill is a rich red. There's a white ring around his neck, and his breast is a handsome reddish brown, speckled with black. He has white sides and wing patches and a dark back. The female is more drab in coloration, but has the distinctive head crest of her partner.

The Redbreasted comes through our region in April and May, headed north to breeding grounds. Nests are hollowed out on the ground, typically under protection of overhanging spruce or fir limbs. The nest is lined with down, and eight to ten or sometimes more buff to olive colored eggs are deposited. The young hatch 26 to 28 days after incubation starts, and as soon as they're dry, they head for water under protection of both parents. They are elusive and wary. When disturbed, the young will scatter into dense cover and remain motionless while the parents attempt to lure away the intruder. Like the loons, these mergansers are able to submerge until only their head is above water, and then can dive quickly out of danger if need arises.

Taking flight from water or land is difficult for the Redbreasted. They must run along for 20 or 30 yards, wings flapping furiously, before they become airborne. In the air, they typically fly at low altitude, and will frequently dive into waves or breakers with a sort of mad abandon. Underwater, they keep wings folded and swim with astonishing speed. On dry land they stand awkwardly, tipped forward or back; or they slide along on their bellies in movement. Partly this is caused by their legs being placed far back on their bodies, typical of fast-swimming divers.

During winter months, Red-breasteds drift south throughout eastern North America to our East and Gulf Coasts, but they also tarry on open water as far north as they can find it, then when warm weather returns they head north again rapidly. Most nesting is in Canada, as far north as the Arctic Circle.

Key Natural History References:
Palmer 1976 v.3, Bellrose 1976,
Johnsgard 1975.

Female

Male

Osprey *Pandion haliaetus*

The Osprey is a flying fish trap. Its major food is fish and it is splendidly equipped for catching them. Its feet are constructed with one of the front toes reversible so that a thrashing fish can be held securely between two talons in front and two in back. Horny projections on the toes further strengthen the Osprey's grip on its dinner. Its sometimes name "Fish Hawk" is well earned.

As would be expected, the Osprey is water-loving, requiring as habitat lakes and streams of clear water where fish are plentiful. It prefers shallow streams and lake shoals where fish swim close to the surface, allowing the Osprey, hovering on beating wings, to see them from 50 to 100 feet overhead. Spotting a fish, it dives abruptly, talons outstretched, and makes off dry-feathered with its dinner.

In size the Osprey is about halfway between eagles and the larger hawks, measuring up to two feet in body length and having a four-and-a-half to six foot wingspread. *It is blackish above with a clear white belly.* There are black wrist marks at the crook of its wing, and broad black patches through its cheeks. Its white head suggests the larger Bald Eagle, though the Osprey is closer in size to a Herring Gull. *At a distance its flexed wing at the wrist joint is a good identification.* Its wingbeats are slow and deep and it reminds one of a Great Blue Heron in flight. It sustains flight by using more wing flapping than sailing. Its call is an annoyed-sounding noisy, sharp cheeping: *"Cheep, Cheep"* or *"Chewk, Chewk"* combined with a whistled throaty *"You, You, You"* and a complaining *"Shriek, Shriek, Shriek."*

Ospreys are monogamous and pairs mate for life. They build large bulky nests of heavy sticks placed in tall dead trees, on rocky ledges, on sand dunes, and even on the crossbars of telephone poles. The primary requirement is a good vantage point higher than the surrounding countryside. A pair usually returns to the same nest year after year, making repairs and additions before the female deposits two to five, typically three, dull white eggs thickly spotted with shades of brown.

The Osprey breeds throughout the world, and nesting habits vary somewhat. In the eastern United States they sometimes nest in loose colonies, but in Michigan the nest sites seem to be more widely separated.

Ospreys get along well with other birds, not bothering them and not being bothered by them except for the fish thievery of the Bald Eagle. It is not unusual for Starlings, English Sparrows, and Grackles to build their own nests in the tangled undersides of Osprey nests.

The Osprey was one of the birds most severely threatened by the widespread use of DDT. But the banning of that pesticide is allowing this bird to slowly increase its numbers in Michigan once again.

After their young are raised, Ospreys leave the Great Lakes region in August to winter in Florida and the Gulf States.

Key Natural History References: Bent 1937, Forbush 1929, Ogden 1975.

Osprey 21-24½ inches

American Black Duck *Anas rubripes*

The common Mallard's closest and most similar relative is the American Black Duck, a dark and plainly colored duck less common and much less inclined to the company of humans than the Mallard. In coloration, the Black Duck and its mate are similar. They are uniformly a dusky brown with lighter yellow-brown head and neck. Both neck and head are finely streaked. A purple wing patch is bordered in black. *In flight the Black Duck is identified by its generally dark body and white underwing linings.* By contrast, the Mallard's body and the underside of the wings are a continuous white, or light color, except for the darker front portion of the breast.

During the nesting season, the male Black Duck will be more commonly seen because he leaves the incubating and raising of young to his mate. Consequently, she is more likely to be hidden in the nest, or among protective marsh grasses at that time. However, there is another difference: the male's bill is greenish yellow; the female's, dark olive-brown.

The identification of Mallards and Black Ducks is not so simple when they interbreed, which they sometimes do. The close relationship between the two species produces hybrid birds which are fertile and so reproduce themselves in a somewhat confusing array of Mallard and Black Duck colors. In one study, it was found that three percent of the Black Ducks showed plumage feathers of both species.

The Black is a wary bird with strong eyesight and hearing, and is not easily coaxed close to humans. Its reputation for caution apparently is sensed by other ducks, for the presence of Blacks on the water usually signals other species that this is a safe place to land.

As with the Mallard, the Black Duck starts its flight from water with a strong spring upward, rising 8 to 10 feet vertically before leveling off downwind. This habit contrasts sharply with the long running start so many other ducks require.

A dabbler, the Black feeds in shallow water, eating the same types of submerged plants and seeds as the Mallard, but varying its diet with acorns and such animal life as mollusks, earthworms, amphibians and fishes.

The Black Duck's nest, however, is quite similar to the Mallard's, but is often well hidden on the ground as far as a mile from water. Its 9 to 10 eggs are creamy-white to greenish-buff. Because the nest is often far away, the young have to complete a long hike to reach water just a few hours after they hatch. For those tender little webbed feet to march a human mile, medals should be given.

Some Black Ducks remain here the year around and can be found on open waters throughout the southern half of our state. In the northern counties, they are typically only seen in the summer. Most wing south to the Gulf of Mexico to spend the cold months in that warmer climate.

Key Natural History References: Bellrose 1976, Palmer 1962, Stotts 1957, Coulter and Miller 1968.

Black Duck 21-25 inches

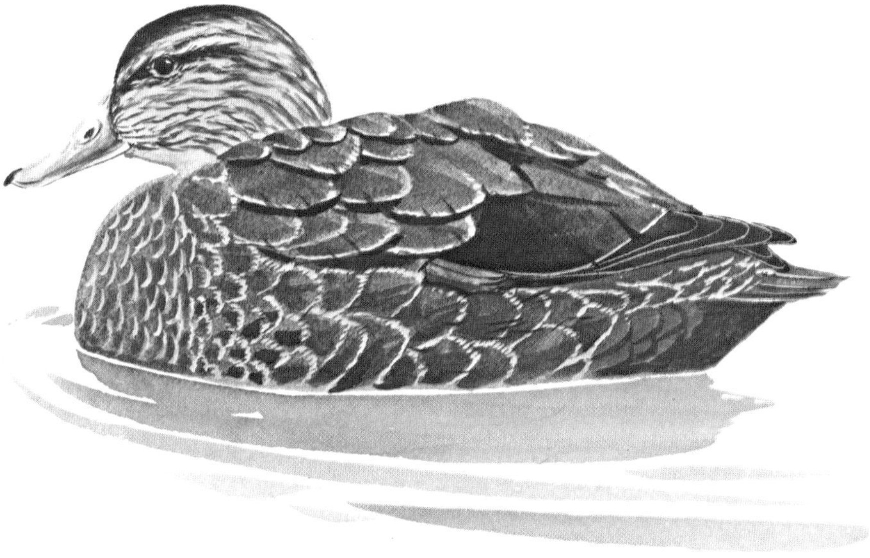

American Bittern *Botaurus lentiginosus*

The American Bittern is the mystery bird of the marshes. It materializes suddenly, as if taking shape from wisps of haze, and flies off slowly over the reeds. Its call comes from deep grass where no form can be seen—in spite of the bird's large size. And it has those wonderful, unusual common names: Thunder Pumper, Shide Poke, Stake Driver.

A large bird which averages nearly two feet in body length, with a wingspan of nearly four feet, the American Bittern is a recluse; you must sneak up on one quietly and even then you may not see this bird as it stands like a statue, absolutely motionless, long beak pointed skyward like a reed, the brown vertical neck stripes blending with other surrounding reeds. But wait patiently, and you may see a hungry Bittern suddenly move to spear a passing fish. Another identifying feature is the flight pattern. If a large brown bird flushes close in front of you on a dense pond or swamp edge, croaks hoarsely, flaps off some distance low over the vegetation and then drops out of sight, it's probably a Bittern.

There is nothing very musical about this big bird's song. Its pneumatic pumping sound is characteristic, and is a call that's made in part by moving the neck grotesquely as the exhaled air passes through the voice box to increase resonance of the call. No other bird makes such a sound. It has been aptly compared to the sucking of an old-fashioned pump when someone tries to raise the water, and as it booms over the marsh its distance and location are hard to determine. That's where the name Thunder Pumper comes from. However, if from a great distance only a single note can be heard, as if someone were driving a stake into soft ground, then it's a Stake Driver.

The Bittern has slate gray wings, a rich brown body color, and a black stripe down the side of its neck. During courting season, the male displays a white ruff, like a white powder puff, at the base of the wings. At other times the ruff is kept concealed beneath surrounding plumage.

The nesting site chosen by the female is always well hidden in the reeds and cattails of a marsh. Dead vegetation is piled from six to twelve inches above the water and it is there that the four or five young are raised among the crawling insects, reptiles, and mammals of the marsh. However, the babies are well protected, for their mother's dagger-like bill and long neck can be lethal, and while still very young they too learn to disappear by remaining motionless.

In summer, this bird may be seen anywhere throughout the Great Lakes region, though it is less common than formerly. In fall, these big birds fly south on long deliberate wing strokes, wings leisurely flexed, to lowlands and marshes of the southern United States. Some may fly on to a few islands of the West Indies.

Key Natural History References:
Palmer 1962, Forbush 1929,
Bent 1926.

Black-crowned Night Heron

Nycticorax nycticorax

A spot of white in a tree far across the pond—where a spot should not be—might be a Black-crowned Night Heron resting from its evening work. While not strictly nocturnal, this large wading bird prefers to feed in the evening hours or after darkness has fallen, or at dawn. But it is also active during the day.

This heron is short and stout with a short thick neck and a chunky body supported by legs which are short by heron standards. Measuring an average of about 26 inches in body length, it is about half the size of the familiar Great Blue Heron. Marked best by its *white breast, black and ashy-gray back, and black crown*—which is slightly crested in breeding plumage, it boasts long white cordlike plumes. The wings are gray and in flight the bird appears to be broadwinged with its feet reaching beyond its tail. The adult is the only whitish heron with a black back. The Black-crowned Night Heron's call is loud and raucous, heard most often in the evening. It is *"Squawk,"* or *"Quawk,"* which has given the bird one of its nicknames.

The major food is that found in and near shallow water: fish, crustaceans, mollusks, worms, insects, reptiles, amphibians, and occasionally young birds and small mammals. It hunts the edges of ponds and marsh pools, often miles from its nest, by moving briskly with head lowered and neck curved, ready to strike. Or it may stand silently waiting for its prey.

Black-crowned Night Herons are gregarious birds, often gathering in large colonies, but just as often they are found singly or in pairs along small bodies of water. In recent years pesticides have taken their toll, for its numbers have diminished, and the large colonies are less common than they once were.

While the bird may nest on the ground or in a bush, or as high as 160 feet up in the top branches of a tree, it typically builds its large nest of loose twigs 20 or 30 feet above the ground. Nesting locations vary considerably, the main requirement usually being a nearness to water. Generally the female lays three to five pale sea-green eggs.

Unlike most herons, this family member flies with its short neck *extended* rather than folded back, looking somewhat like a gull flying over the water with its deliberate wing strokes.

Winters are spent over a wide territory and in a variety of climates, which place it anywhere from southern New England to California and south to South America. However, it is not present in the Great Lakes region during the cold months.

Key Natural History References: Palmer 1962, Forbush 1929, Bent 1926, Noble et al. 1938.

136

Black-crowned Night Heron 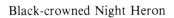   23-28 inches

Herring Gull *Larus argentatus*

Herring Gulls are familiar to everyone who has spent any time along our Great Lakes shores. They are common on larger inland waters as well, foraging on plowed fields or winging along over rivers or lakes when the Great Lakes are whipped by big winds.

The Herring Gull is the largest of Michigan's two common gulls, having *a body about two feet long. Mature birds have an over-all light gray color, a pure white head, chest, and tail, and black wingtips. The legs are pink.* The young in their first winter are a fairly uniform brown. By the second winter they have turned or have white mixed with brown in a somewhat speckled fashion. They look more like the adults at that point, but retain a black tip to their tail feathers through the third winter. In their fourth year they finally emerge in the white plumage of the adult.

Both the Herring Gull and Michigan's other familiar gull, the Ringbill, love to soar like hawks on high thermal air currents. They also are seen frequently standing motionless on sand bars, dock bollards, boathouse roofs, and other shoreline promontories. Sometimes they bob in rafts of hundreds far out from shore on the Great Lakes. At other times they wheel about behind fishing boats in raucous excitement at the promise of food. At lake resorts they gather quickly and boldly when youngsters throw them bread or any of the variety of foods which appeal to their scavenger appetites. Herring Gulls are especially fond of carrion which washes up along beaches, and they are often regulars at garbage dumps far inland. Current laws which require daily burial of such material at public landfills have reduced this habit sharply, however. One interesting habit is a reported technique of opening clam shells by dropping them from a height to crack the shell. Their bills are long and strong and have a slight hook on the end. Carrion is eaten bones and all, with the indigestable residue spit out in pellets similar to the habit of owls. This rugged digestive system and eat-anything appetite make the Herring Gull well equipped for survival.

This bird's call, a loud bugled *"Koo-ow, Kee-ow,"* accompanied by much whining, squealing, and mewing, is a part of the very atmosphere of the Great Lakes shorelines. In nesting colonies, the call is a dry *"gah-gah-gah."*

The nesting colonies are established on remote sand spits or uninhabited islands. Nests are set close together, with scores of birds making up a typical colony. Two or three eggs are laid, from which the ungainly young soon appear. In winter, some Herring Gulls remain here where they can find open water, while others migrate southward, some traveling as far as the Gulf of Mexico.

Key Natural History References: Bent 1932, Pough 1951, Payne 1983.

Turkey Vulture *Cathartes aura*

Close up, the Turkey Vulture, even by the most generous measures, has to be considered a somewhat ugly bird. It smells bad, it is clumsy on the ground, it lives on dead creatures, and it goes by the unattractive nickname of "Buzzard." Yet it is one of our most graceful soaring birds, and as that is when you'll most likely see it, you may well enjoy the encounter.

From early March until fall, this large dark colored bird soars effortlessly on its nearly six-foot wingspan over the entire Great Lakes region countryside in a constant search for food, relying in that quest on excellent sight, its sense of smell, and the occasional circling congregations of other Turkey Vultures. These flight habits allow the Vulture to observe an enormous area, and few changes in the landscape escape its vision. It does this with very minimum effort, and so controls its output of energy carefully. It climbs high on warm air updrafts, and seems to take advantage of every current of wind to *soar and circle on usually motionless wings. Even in strong winds, it soars and sweeps with the V of its wings turning steadily and surely*. The wings are wide and set far forward so that the head and neck, when seen in flight, appear small compared to other soaring birds, such as the hawks. The body and wings are a uniform dark gray with black coverts when seen from below.

The Turkey Vulture has a large hooked beak, well designed to tear flesh. Its weaker feet, however, cannot capture live food as readily as other birds of prey and so it feeds mostly on decaying flesh. The arrival of automobiles in this century was one of the most important developments for Turkey Vultures because of the unending supply of road kills that they now provide as food to these big birds. *Its head and neck are bare of plumage*, giving it the characteristic turkey-like appearance.

It lays two buffy or greenish white eggs blotched with brown or purple in a nest carelessly scraped together in hollow logs, under stumps, or in caves or niches among rocks on bluffs and overlooks. It feeds its ungainly young by regurgitating partially digested carrion, so the nesting area becomes as unpleasant to human intruders as the Vulture's general lifestyle. While the young hiss when disturbed at the nest, the adult goes through life nearly soundless. The Turkey Vulture may be nature's scavenger, but it redeems itself in the eyes of birdwatchers who thrill to its swift gliding on spring winds, and its effortless soaring on the warm air of summer days. At night, the birds will commonly roost together in large clusters, where they remain until late enough in the mornings for the sun to heat the earth and start the updrafts of warm air on which they soar so effortlessly.

Turkey Vultures soar away to our southern states and to Central America to spend the winter months.

Key Natural History References:
Bent 1937, Forbush and May 1939,
Todd 1940, Kempton 1927, Work and
Wool 1942.

Common Loon *Gavia immer*

Perhaps no bird is more symbolic of northern wilderness than the Loon. Its impressive size, its command of northern lakes and its wild wolf-like call all say "Northwoods" to those who look forward to seeing it on vacations throughout the upper Great Lakes region. When a Loon appears, it is never hard to imagine days past when packs of wolves ran free and Indian canoes slipped along on quiet waters. The Loon evokes such thoughts.

About the size of a small Canada Goose, *the Common Loon is most readily recognized by its large glossy greenish-black head and the checkered black and white pattern on its back. It has a stout tapered bill, the upper part of which is also black. Its red eyes* can be seen through binoculars, or when out of curiosity it swims near enough to be seen in detail.

When the Loon flies, it can be identified from other large water birds by the downward curve of its neck.

The cry of the Loon is truly wild, a maniacal *"ha-ha-ha"* or a *"hoo-loooo,"* a sort of yodel which echoes back from a lake's shores, as the howl of the wolf once did. It is heard most often at night and in stormy weather, settings which tend to make the hair stand up on the startled listener's neck. It is a weird, uncanny sound, and one of the most haunting heard in the north country.

Almost completely a water bird, the Common Loon is clumsy on dry land where it must use both feet and wings to skid itself along on its breast. But in the water it is thoroughly at home. It lives almost entirely on fish which it spots by holding its head underwater, and then pursues the hapless fish at high speed, using its wings to aid in its powerful swimming. Loons can travel great distances under water, diving when threatened and breathing by thrusting only their bills above the surface. At times they are seen swimming with only their heads above water, looking like miniature submarines.

Loons nest on a collection of floating water vegetation, or often on small islands and frequently on muskrat houses, where they hollow out a simple depression. Two olive-brown eggs spotted with brown and black are laid, always at a place where the nesting bird is able to leave the nest quickly by sliding into the water. For the first weeks, the young often ride on their parents' backs, miniature balls of fluff hanging on for dear life. The family takes to the water early to spend most of its life there, sleeping on the water or at its edge, ready to dive instantly at the first sight of danger. When taking off, this heavy-bodied bird must make long runs along the water, feet and wings beating, head thrust forward, as it picks up speed.

It alights, however, at high speed in sharp, abrupt dives. Loons leave the northern Great Lakes region in winter, and spend the cold months along the Gulf and south Atlantic coasts.

Key Natural History References: Palmer 1962, Vermeer 1973, Bent 1919, Hammond and Wood 1977.

Winter

Summer

Bald Eagle *Haliaeetus leucocephalus*

For 200 years this magnificent bird has served as our national emblem, and the wisdom of its choice for that role has been heightened by time. It is large, majestic, and dignified, and sighting one in the wild these days is an event to be talked about and remembered.

Michigan is fortunate to be included in the habitat of this colorful bird. It is infrequently seen throughout the state, both during its migration and at its nests in isolated spots, primarily now along our Lake Michigan coast and in the Upper Peninsula. *The mature adult is instantly recognized because of its nearly three foot body length, its seven foot wingspread, and, of course, its white head and tail.* Immature Bald Eagles lack the white head, and they are somewhat larger than the adult.

Bald Eagles mate for life and stay together until one dies. Pairs may occasionally be seen, perched together so closely that their two bodies touch. They return year after year to the same nest, each spring adding more material to what grows to be a huge platform of sticks, sometimes six feet in diameter and typically four feet or more in height. Such continued use causes the nest to grow, and one old one was measured to be 8½ feet across and 12 feet deep. Such nests are built in the tops of the most commanding tree in the wild neighborhood, usually white pines in Michigan. There, one to three dull white eggs are laid and hatched and the long period of feeding the young begins.

The adults seldom travel far from the nest during this growth period, even after the young are out trying their wings among the limbs of the nest tree. The parents are either soaring high overhead or sitting motionless watching for food within the range of their field of vision.

Food for Bald Eagles consists primarily of fish which they pluck from the water or steal from Ospreys and other fish-eating birds. They also feed on carrion, especially dead fish they find along lakes and streams. Occasionally they feed on mammals and smaller birds such as gulls and terns, but their main diet is fish.

The Bald Eagle is an unusually strong flier and physically powerful bird, but tales of babies and grown sheep being stolen are only tales. Even though it is so widely admired, the Bald Eagles's main enemy has long been humans, who have killed them with guns and more recently with habitat destruction and pesticides. But prison terms imposed for killing eagles and the control of pesticides in the environment are resulting in more eagles in areas where they can find the sort of great solitude they seem to need in order to prosper. Consequently, its loud scream, the young's *"Pee-Pee-e-Pee,"* the clear *"Kak-Kak-Kak,"* and the maniacal laugh of the adult are being heard more frequently once again in our region.

Key Natural History References: Bent 1937, Forbush 1929, Broley 1947.

144

Bald Eagle   *30-43 inches*

Sandhill Crane *Grus canadensis*

One's first sighting of a Sandhill Crane is not easily forgotten. No matter if the bird is flying, or standing quietly on an open hillside, the Sandhill is a magnificent bird, one of the largest in the Great Lakes region. It is the state's only Crane, the only similar species being the smaller Great Blue Heron.

The Sandhill is distinctive in many ways. *Its plumage is gray or brown, never bluish, and its bald forehead is red bumpy bird skin. Another mark is the tuft of long inner wing feathers which droop over the tail. Its bill is shorter and heavier than a heron's and its body—above those long spindly legs—stockier. In flight the Sandhill's neck is fully extended, the most definite way of distinguishing this bird from the herons, whose necks curve back in a long "S" during flight.*

A flight of these four-foot tall birds, necks extended, long stick-like legs trailing, 80-inch wingspan beating powerful downstokes and rapid upstrokes, would be exciting enough if the Crane were silent. But flight often is accompanied by their loud, resonant cries which carry great distances. The call has been described as a *"K-r-r-o-o-o, K-r-r-o-o-o,"* wild trumpeting, high and eerie, which can be heard long after the bird has disappeared. On high dry ground, where the Crane frequently nests, rests and feeds, it moves with measured pace, gracefully and, if need be, rapidly. It is watchful and because of its height and open habitat, it sees all and is difficult to approach.

The spring courtship "dance" is a frenzied activity in which several males will walk about slowly with heads high in the air, then suddenly lower heads to the ground and bounce about in criss-crossing circles, leaping up from the ground sometimes with wings raised, sometimes with wings drooping, their speed growing into a blur until finally, by some unknown signal, the dance ends.

Sandhills nest on the ground in slight depressions lined with grass. Two large eggs are laid, sometimes in low areas well protected by tall grasses, or along marsh edges.

Even though they are waders, Sandhill Cranes seem to spend a great deal of time on high ground in open areas, such as burned-over openings, sand hills, and meadows throughout the Great Lakes region. Their diet is a variety of foods: roots, bulbs, grain, mice, frogs, lizards, snakes and insects.

This varied diet makes them fat birds in late summer and, as a result, the Sandhill at one time was hunted so extensively it was nearly eliminated from our region. But with protection this giant among the state's birds has come back slowly but steadily. In spring and fall, the watcher can expect to see migrating family units, flying high in their straight goose-like formations, periodically announcing their loud unforgettable call, on their way to or from our region. The cold months are spent in the Gulf States and south to Mexico.

Key Natural History References: Bent 1926, Walkinshaw 1973.

Sandhill Crane

40-48 inches

Wild Turkey *Meleagris gallopavo*

The Wild Turkey is so much a part of the American tradition that it hardly seems a "bird" at all. It is part of every Indian, Pilgrim, and pioneer story, every Thanksgiving, and most bucolic barnyard scenes. We all cherish the story of Benjamin Franklin's burning and strongly justified desire to make it our national symbol, rather than the Bald Eagle.

But the Wild Turkey, now beginning to increase in numbers throughout wooded areas of the central Great Lakes region, is a different bird than the one we eat at Thanksgiving, and then make use of in sandwiches for days after.

It is, for example, a much slimmer bird, and has chestnut colored tips to its tail feathers, marking it as the wild bird, just as white tips identify the domestic. But even that distinction fades as wild and barnyard birds often interbreed. The male—the gobbler—is an impressive 48 inches in body size, from the end of its bill to the tip of its tail. The female is a full foot shorter.

At the turn of the century the Turkey was considered extinct in our Great Lakes region, but re-introduction of birds from Pennsylvania into southern Michigan forests proved successful, and the Turkey has since thrived in forests all over the southern Great Lakes region. Today it is so numerous that limited hunting seasons are allowed, under a lottery-permit system. The gobbler's call is the familiar chattery "*gobble, obble-obble-obble*" or a plaintive "*keow-keow-keow*" which can be heard in open woodlands and clearings in early morning as the male calls his harem together.

Turkeys roost in trees, and although they are swift fliers, they appear to dislike flying very far and prefer to run hell-bent through thick ground cover rather than fly when alarmed. They move through forest areas in small family flocks, feeding on acorns, fruit, and seeds, scratching and pecking as they go, just as their barnyard cousin does. Nests are built on the ground where large clutches of from 10 to 18 eggs, buff colored and thinly speckled with brown, are laid. The hen takes sole charge of the chicks, which leave the nest with her soon after hatching.

The Turkey is now widespread in the southern reaches of the Great Lakes region, though few residents see them. *The male Turkey has a head covered with bumpy bare skin and fleshy wattles, all in a patriotic mix of red, white and blue. A coarse tuft of long black bristles, called a beard, grows from the central chest of the gobbler, and hens sometimes also exhibit shorter tufts. The over-all plumage is dark brown in metallic iridescent shades of bronze, copper, blued steel, and gold, all varying according to the light in which the bird is seen.* A year-round resident in its chosen habitat, the Turkey winters near where it nests, and probably spends its entire life in a two or three mile wide circle.

Key Natural History References: Bent 1932, Schorger 1966, Mosby and Handley 1943.

Wild Turkey

36 inches (Female)
48 inches (Male)

Male

Great Blue Heron *Ardea herodias*

The Great Blue Heron is an ungainly bird which does very graceful things. *One of Michigan's largest birds, it may stand four feet in height and has a six foot wingspan. On the ground, its body appears to teeter on long stilt-like legs. Its neck is long, supporting a relatively large head and a strong dagger-like bill.*

There is something of a gangly Ichabod Crane about this spindly bird, but when it flies or stalks through the water it is a picture of grace.

There are Herons which are more blue in color than the Great Blue, yet it must be noted that a slight bluish cast to the dark gray body feathers does appear. This heron's head and the underside of the neck are both whitish, and there are other color subtleties about this bird usually not quickly apparent to a casual watcher crouched beside a pond. *Size and general gray color are the best identification features.*

A carnivorous bird, the Great Blue Heron spends long hours hunting and fishing to support its big body. It stands motionless in shallow water watching for frogs and fish, or wades smoothly and silently as it hunts. When prey is spotted, the long neck drives the bill to its target so quickly the motion seems more imagined than real.

Perhaps because of its height, allowing it to see above the surrounding reeds, the Heron is difficult to approach closely. Often the first glimpse comes when it leaps awkwardly into the air and sails off on powerful, slow wingbeats. As it gains speed and altitude, often circling back above the treetops, the Great Blue's flight is impressive and exciting to watch.

Solitary during most of the year, this heron is social in its nesting habits. Audubon described the courtship as a gathering of a large number of both males and females in one location, where the males charged at one another, running along the ground with wings outspread, knifing at each other with their long bills. The females stood nearby, "uttering coaxing notes." Audubon said this display continued for a time until somehow the pairings were decided and pairs departed for the nesting sites. The Great Blue builds huge, semi-permanent tree nests composed of sticks, constructed in the company of its kind, in colonies called heronries. Stands of isolated large trees are preferred, though they are less common in our region than they once were. The locations of such colonies are often a secret pleasure of the lucky birdwatchers who find them. The birds lay three to six greenish blue eggs and frequently travel long distances between their feeding grounds and their hungry young. Great Blue Herons are common in Michigan during the summer months. Although a few stay behind in winter where open water remains, most migrate to the Ohio Valley, our southern states, and to the West Indies, Panama, and Venezuela.

Key Natural History References: Palmer 1962, Pratt 1970, Bent 1926.

Checklist Of Birds In This Book

☐ BITTERN, AMERICAN
Botaurus lentiginosus
When _____
Where _____

☐ BOBWHITE, COMMON
Colinus virginianus
When _____
Where _____

☐ CHAT, YELLOW-BREASTED
Icteria virens
When _____
Where _____

☐ COOT, AMERICAN
Fulica americana
When _____
Where _____

☐ CRANE, SANDHILL
Grus canadensis
When _____
Where _____

☐ CROSSBILL, RED
Loxia curvirostra
When _____
Where _____

☐ CROW, AMERICAN
Corvus brachyrhynchos
When _____
Where _____

☐ DUCK, AMERICAN BLACK
Anas rubripes
When _____
Where _____

☐ DUCK, BUFFLEHEAD
Bucephala albeola
When _____
Where _____

☐ DUCK, CANVASBACK
Aythya valisineria
When _____
Where _____

☐ DUCK, REDHEAD
Aythya americana
When _____
Where _____

☐ DUCK, RING-NECKED
Aythya collaris
When _____
Where _____

☐ DUCK, WOOD
Aix sponsa
When _____
Where _____

☐ EAGLE, BALD
Haliaeetus leucocephalus
When _____
Where _____

☐ FLYCATCHER, YELLOW-BELLIED
Empidonax flaviventris
When _____
Where _____

☐ GALLINULE, COMMON
Gallinula chloropus
When _____
Where _____

☐ GOLDENEYE, COMMON
Bucephala clangula
When _____
Where _____

☐ GREBE, PIED-BILLED
Podilymbus podiceps
When _____
Where _____

☐ GROUSE, RUFFED
Bonasa umbellus
When _____
Where _____

☐ GROUSE, SPRUCE
Canachites canadensis
When _____
Where _____

☐ GULL, HERRING
Larus argentatus
When _____
Where _____

☐ GULL, RING-BILLED
Larus delawarensis
When _____
Where _____

☐ HARRIER, NORTHERN
Circus cyaneus
When _____
Where _____

☐ HAWK, COOPER'S
Accipiter cooperii
When _____
Where _____

☐ HAWK, RED-TAILED
Buteo jamaicensis
When _____
Where _____

☐ HAWK, SHARP-SHINNED
Accipiter striatus
When _____
Where _____

☐ HERON, BLACK-CROWNED NIGHT
Nycticorax nycticorax
When _____
Where _____

☐ HERON, GREAT BLUE
Ardea herodias
When _____
Where _____

☐ HERON, GREEN
Butorides striatus
When _____
Where _____

☐ JAY, GRAY
Perisoreus canadensis
When _____
Where _____

☐ KESTREL, AMERICAN
Falco sparverius
When _____
Where _____

☐ KILLDEER
Charadrius vociferus
When _____
Where _____

☐ KINGFISHER, BELTED
Megaceryle alcyon
When _____
Where _____

☐ LOON, COMMON
Gavia immer
When _____
Where _____

☐ MEADOWLARK, EASTERN
Sturnella magna
When _____
Where _____

☐ MERGANSER, RED-BREASTED
Mergus serrator
When _____
Where _____

☐ NIGHTHAWK, COMMON
Chordeiles minor
When _____
Where _____

☐ OSPREY
Pandion haliaetus
When _____
Where _____

☐ OWL, BARN
Tyto alba
When _____
Where _____

☐ OWL, BARRED
Strix varia
When _____
Where _____

☐ OWL, COMMON SCREECH
Otus asio
When _____
Where _____

☐ OWL, GREAT HORNED
Bubo virginianus
When _____
Where _____

☐ PLOVER, BLACK-BELLIED
Pluvialis squatarola
When _____
Where _____

☐ PLOVER, PIPING
Charadrius melodus
When _____
Where _____

☐ PLOVER, SEMIPALMATED
Charadrius semipalmatus
When _____
Where _____

☐ RAVEN, NORTHERN
Corvus corax
When _____
Where _____

☐ SANDERLING
Calidris alba
When _____
Where _____

☐ SANDPIPER, SEMIPALMATED
Calidris pusilla
When _____
Where _____

☐ SANDPIPER, SOLITARY
Tringa solitaria
When _____
Where _____

☐ SANDPIPER, SPOTTED
Actitis macularia
When _____
Where _____

☐ SANDPIPER, UPLAND
Bartramia longicauda
When _____
Where _____

☐ SCAUP, GREATER
Aythya marila
When _____
Where _____

☐ SCAUP, LESSER
Aythya affinis
When _____
Where _____

☐ SHRIKE, LOGGERHEAD
Lanius ludovicianus
When _____
Where _____

☐ SHRIKE, NORTHERN
Lanius excubitor
When _____
Where _____

☐ SNIPE, COMMON
Capella gallinago
When _____
Where _____

☐ SORA
Porzana carolina
When _____
Where _____

☐ SPARROW, VESPER
Pooecetes gramineus
When _____
Where _____

☐ SWALLOW, BANK
Riparia riparia
When _____
Where _____

☐ TEAL, BLUE-WINGED
Anas discors
When _____
Where _____

☐ TEAL, GREEN-WINGED
Anas crecca
When _____
Where _____

☐ TERN, BLACK
Chlidonias niger
When _____
Where _____

☐ TERN, COMMON
Sterna hirundo
When _____
Where _____

☐ TURKEY, WILD
Meleagris gallopavo
When _____
Where _____

☐ VIREO, WARBLING
Vireo gilvus
When _____
Where _____

☐ VULTURE, TURKEY
Cathartes aura
When _____
Where _____

☐ WARBLER, BAY-BREASTED
Dendroica castanea
When _____
Where _____

☐ WARBLER, BLACKBURNIAN
Dendroica fusca
When _____
Where _____

☐ WARBLER, BLACKPOLL
Dendroica striata
When _____
Where _____

☐ WARBLER, BLACK-THROATED GREEN
Dendroica virens
When _____
Where _____

☐ WARBLER, MAGNOLIA
Dendroica magnolia
When _____
Where _____

☐ WARBLER, PALM
Dendroica palmarum
When _____
Where _____

☐ WARBLER, PINE
Dendroica pinus
When _____
Where _____

☐ WARBLER, PROTHONOTARY
Protonotaria citrea
When _____
Where _____

☐ WHIP-POOR-WILL
Caprimulgus vociferus
When _____
Where _____

☐ WOODCOCK, AMERICAN
Philohela minor
When _____
Where _____

☐ WOODPECKER, PILEATED
Dryocopus pileatus
When _____
Where _____

☐ WREN, WINTER
Troglodytes troglodytes
When _____
Where _____

☐ YELLOWLEGS, GREATER
Tringa melanoleuca
When _____
Where _____

☐ YELLOWLEGS, LESSER
Tringa flavipes
When _____
Where _____

Checklist Of All Michigan Birds

The following list of 406 birds known to nest or migrate through or visit Michigan was compiled by Robert B. Payne of the University of Michigan's Museum of Zoology. It represents records of museum specimens, field observations, photos, and tape recordings through early 1982, and extending back to earliest reports. You'll note in a handful of cases differences of common names for some species; the book itself listing one name, the checklist another. Species in the book follow the earlier, more commonly known, species names established by the American Ornithologists' Union (AOU) prior to about 1975; checklist includes changes made in the last 8 to 10 years, and in use primarily by specialists.

____Anhinga
____Ani, Groove-billed
____Ani, Smooth-billed
____Avocet, American
____Bittern, American
____Bittern, Least
____Blackbird, Brewer's
____Blackbird, Red-winged
____Blackbird, Rusty
____Blackbird, Yellow-headed
____Bluebird, Eastern
____Bluebird, Mountain
____Bobolink
____Bobwhite, Northern
____Brant
____Bufflehead
____Bunting, Indigo
____Bunting, Lark
____Bunting, Painted
____Bunting, Snow
____Canvasback
____Caracara, Crested
____Cardinal, Northern
____Catbird, Gray
____Chat, Yellow-breasted
____Chickadee, Black-capped
____Chickadee, Boreal
____Chickadee, Carolina
____Chuck-will's widow
____Coot, American
____Cormorant, Double-crested
____Cowbird, Brown-headed
____Crane, Sandhill
____Creeper, Brown
____Crow, American
____Crossbill, Red

____Crossbill, White-winged
____Cuckoo, Black-billed
____Cuckoo, yellow-billed
____Curlew, Eskimo
____Curlew, Long-billed
____Dickcissel
____Dove, Common Ground
____Dove, Mourning
____Dove, Rock
____Dovekie
____Dowitcher, Long-billed
____Dowitcher, Short-billed
____Duck, American Black
____Duck, Black-bellied Whistling
____Duck, Fulvous Whistling
____Duck, Harlequin
____Duck, Ring-necked
____Duck, Ruddy
____Duck, Tufted
____Duck, Wood
____Dunlin
____Eagle, Bald
____Eagle, Golden
____Egret, Cattle
____Egret, Great
____Egret, Snowy
____Eider, Common
____Eider, King
____Falcon, Peregrine
____Falcon, Prairie
____Finch, House
____Finch, Purple
____Finch, Rosy
____Flamingo, Greater

____Flicker, Northern
____Flycatcher, Acadian
____Flycatcher, Alder
____Flycatcher, Great Crested
____Flycatcher, Least
____Flycatcher, Olive-sided
____Flycatcher, Scissor-tailed
____Flycatcher, Vermillion
____Flycatcher, Willow
____Flycatcher, Yellow-bellied
____Gadwall
____Gallinule, Purple
____Gannet, Northern
____Gannet, Blue-gray
____Godwit, Hudsonian
____Godwit, Marbled
____Goldeneye, Barrow's
____Goldeneye, Common
____Goldfinch, American
____Goldfinch, European
____Goose, Bar-headed
____Goose, Barnacle
____Goose, Canada
____Goose, Greater White-fronted
____Goose, Ross'
____Goose, Snow
____Goshawk, Northern
____Grackle, Common
____Grebe, Eared
____Grebe, Horned
____Grebe, Pied-billed
____Grebe, Red-necked
____Grebe, Western
____Grosbeak, Black-headed
____Grosbeak, Blue

____Grosbeak, Evening
____Grosbeak, Pine
____Grosbeak,
    Rose-breasted
____Grouse, Ruffed
____Grouse, Sharp-tailed
____Grouse, Spruce
____Gull, Bonaparte's
____Gull, California
____Gull, Common
    Black-headed
____Gull, Franklin's
____Gull, Glaucous
____Gull, Glaucous-winged
____Gull, Great
    Black-backed
____Gull, Heermann's
____Gull, Herring
____Gull, Iceland
____Gull, Ivory
____Gull, Laughing
____Gull, Lesser
    Black-backed
____Gull, Little
____Gull, Mew
____Gull, Ring-billed
____Gull, Sabine's
____Gull, Thayer's
____Gyrfalcon
____Harrier, Northern
____Hawk, Broad-winged
____Hawk, Cooper's
____Hawk, Ferruginous
____Hawk,
    Red-shouldered
____Hawk, Red-tailed
____Hawk, Rough-legged
____Hawk, Sharp-shinned
____Hawk, Swainson's
____Heron, Black-crowned
____Heron, Great Blue
____Heron, Green
____Heron, Little Blue
____Heron, Louisiana
____Heron, Yellow-
    crowned Night
____Hummingbird,
    Ruby-throated
____Hummingbird, Rufous
____Ibis, Glossy
____Ibis, White
____Ibis, White-faced
____Jaeger, Long-tailed
____Jaeger, Parasitic
____Jaeger, Pomarine
____Jay, Blue
____Jay, Gray
____Junco, Dark-eyed

____Kestrel, American
____Killdeer
____Kingbird, Eastern
____Kingbird, Western
____Kingfisher, Belted
____Kinglet,
    Golden-crowned
____Kinglet,
    Ruby-crowned
____Kite, American
    Swallow-tailed
____Kite, Black-shouldered
____Kite, Mississippi
____Kittiwake,
    Black-legged
____Knot, Red
____Lark, Horned
____Longspur,
    Chestnut-collared
____Longspur, Lapland
____Longspur, McCown's
____Longspur, Smith's
____Loon, Common
____Loon, Red-throated
____Magpie, Black-billed
____Mallard
____Martin, Purple
____Meadowlark, Eastern
____Meadowlark, Western
____Merganser, Common
____Merganser, Hooded
____Merganser,
    Red-breasted
____Merlin
____Mockingbird,
    Northern
____Moorhen, Common
____Murre, Thick-billed
____Murrelet, Ancient
____Nighthawk, Common
____Nutcracker, Clarke's
____Nuthatch,
    Red-breasted
____Nuthatch,
    White-breasted
____Oldsquaw
____Oriole, Audubon's
____Oriole, Hooded
____Oriole, Northern
____Oriole, Orchard
____Osprey
____Ovenbird
____Owl, Barred
____Owl, Boreal
____Owl, Burrowing
____Owl, Common Barn
____Owl, Eastern Screech
____Owl, Great Gray

____Owl, Great Horned
____Owl, Long-eared
____Owl, Northern Hawk
____Owl, Northern
    Saw-whet
____Owl, Short-eared
____Owl, Snowy
____Parakeet, Carolina
____Parakeet, Monk
____Partridge, Gray
____Parula, Northern
____Pelican, American
    White
____Pelican, Brown
____Phalarope, Red
____Phalarope, Red-
    necked
____Phalarope, Wilson's
____Pheasant, Ring-necked
____Phoebe, Eastern
____Phoebe, Say's
____Pigeon, Band-tailed
____Pigeon, Passenger
____Pintail, Northern
____Pipit, Sprague's
____Pipit, Water
____Plover, Black-bellied
____Plover, Lesser Golden
____Plover, Piping
____Plover, Semipalmated
____Plover, Snowy
____Prairie Chicken,
    Greater
____Ptarmigan, Willow
____Rail, black
____Rail, King
____Rail, Virginia
____Rail, Yellow
____Raven, Common
____Redhead
____Redpoll, Common
____Redpoll, Hoary
____Redstart, American
____Robin, American
____Ruff
____Sanderling
____Sandpiper, Baird's
____Sandpiper,
    Buff-breasted
____Sandpiper, Curlew
____Sandpiper, Least
____Sandpiper, Pectoral
____Sandpiper, Purple
____Sandpiper,
    Semipalmated
____Sandpiper, Solitary
____Sandpiper, Spotted
____Sandpiper, Stilt

____Sandpiper, Upland
____Sandpiper, Western
____Sandpiper,
    White-rumped
____Sapsucker,
    Yellow-bellied
____Scaup, Greater
____Scaup, Lesser
____Scoter, Black
____Scoter, Surf
____Scoter, White-winged
____Shoveler, Northern
____Shrike, Loggerhead
____Shrike, Northern
____Siskin, Pine
____Skimmer, Black
____Snipe, Common
____Solitaire, Townsend's
____Sora
____Sparrow, American
    Tree
____Sparrow, Bachman's
____Sparrow, Chipping
____Sparrow, Clay-colored
____Sparrow, Field
____Sparrow, Fox
____Sparrow,
    Golden-crowned
____Sparrow, Grasshopper
____Sparrow, Harris'
____Sparrow, Henslow's
____Sparrow, House
____Sparrow, Lark
____Sparrow, Le Conte's
____Sparrow, Lincoln's
____Sparrow, Savannah
____Sparrow, Sharp-tailed
____Sparrow, Song
____Sparrow, Swamp
____Sparrow, Vesper
____Sparrow,
    White-crowned
____Sparrow,
    White-throated
____Starling, European
____Stilt, Black-necked
____Stork, Wood
____Swallow, Bank
____Swallow, Barn
____Swallow, Cliff
____Swallow, Northern
    Rough-winged
____Swallow, Tree
____Swan, Mute
____Swan, Trumpeter
____Swan, Tundra
____Swift, Chimney
____Swift, White-throated

____Tanager, Scarlet
____Tanager, Summer
____Tanager, Western
____Teal, blue-winged
____Teal, Cinnamon
____Teal, Green-winged
____Tern, Arctic
____Tern, Black
____Tern, Caspian
____Tern, Common
____Tern, Forster's
____Tern, Least
____Thrasher, Brown
____Thrasher, Curve-billed
____Thrush, Gray-cheeked
____Thrush, Hermit
____Thrush, Swainson's
____Thrush, Varied
____Thrush, Wood
____Titmouse, Tufted
____Towhee, Green-tailed
____Towhee, Rufous-sided
____Turkey, Wild
____Turnstone, Ruddy
____Veery
____Vireo, Bell's
____Vireo, Philadelphia
____Vireo, Red-eyed
____Vireo, Solitary
____Vireo, Warbling
____Vireo, White-eyed
____Vireo, Yellow-throated
____Vulture, Black
____Vulture, Turkey
____Warbler, Bay-breasted
____Warbler,
    Black-and-white
____Warbler, Black-
    throated Blue
____Warbler, Black-
    throated Gray
____Warbler, Black-
    throated Green
____Warbler, Blackburnian
____Warbler, Blackpoll
____Warbler, Blue-winged
____Warbler, Canada
____Warbler, Cape May
____Warbler, Cerulean
____Warbler,
    Chestnut-sided
____Warbler, Connecticut
____Warbler,
    Golden-winged
____Warbler, Hooded
____Warbler, Kentucky
____Warbler, Kirtland's
____Warbler, Magnolia

____Warbler, Mourning
____Warbler, Nashville
____Warbler,
    Orange-crowned
____Warbler, Palm
____Warbler, Pine
____Warbler, Prairie
____Warbler,
    Prothonotary
____Warbler, Tennessee
____Warbler, Wilson's
____Warbler, Worm-eating
____Warbler, Yellow
____Warbler,
    Yellow-rumped
____Warbler,
    Yellow-throated
____Waterthrush,
    Louisiana
____Waterthrush,
    Northern
____Waxwing, Bohemian
____Waxwing, Cedar
____Wheatear, Northern
____Whimbrel,
____Whip-poor-will
____Wigeon, American
____Wigeon, Eurasian
____Willet
____Wood-pewee, Eastern
____Woodcock, American
____Woodpecker,
    Black-backed
____Woodpecker, Downy
____Woodpecker,
    Golden-fronted
____Woodpecker, Hairy
____Woodpecker, Lewis
____Woodpecker, Pileated
____Woodpecker,
    Red-bellied
____Woodpecker,
    Red-cockaded
____Woodpecker, Red-
    headed
____Woodpecker,
    Three-toed
____Wren, Bewick's
____Wren, Carolina
____Wren, House
____Wren, Marsh
____Wren, Rock
____Wren, Sedge
____Wren, Winter
____Yellowlegs, Greater
____Yellowlegs, Lesser
____Yellowthroat,
    Common

Bibliography

Armstrong, E.A., 1956. Territory in the wren. Ibis 98:430-437.

Armstrong, J.T., 1965. Breeding home range in the nighthawk and other birds. Ecology 46(5):619-629.

Balgooyen, T.G. 1976. Behavior and ecology of the American kestrel. Univ. Cal. Publ. Zool. 103:1-83.

Bellrose, F.C., 1976. Ducks, geese, and swans of N. America. Stackpole Books, Harrisburg, PA. 540p.

Bennett, L.J., 1938. The Blue-winged Teal. Collegiate Press, Ames, Iowa. 144p.

Bent, A.C., Life Histories of North American Birds, in 26 volumes. First published as bulletins of the National Museum from 1919 through 1968, and subsequently published by Dover Press, New York as a series of paperbacks, some of which are still available from that publisher.

Beyer, L.K., 1938. Nest life of the bank swallow. Wilson Bull. 50:22-137.

Broley, C.L., 1947. Migration and nesting of Florida bald eagles. Wilson Bull. 59:3-20.

Bryant, L., Jr., 1931. Some notes on the breeding of the vesper sparrow. Bird-banding 2:178-184.

Bull, E., 1975. Habitat utilization of the pileated woodpecker...M.S. Thesis, Oregon State U. 58p.

Bump, G., et. al., 1947. The ruffed grouse. New York Cons. Dept. 896p.

Buss, I.O. & Hawkins, A.S., 1939. The upland plover at...Wisconsin. Wilson Bull. 51(4):202-220.

Cade, T.C., 1967. Ecological and behavioral aspects of predation by the northern shrike. The Living Bird 6:43-86.

Carter, B.C., 1958. The American goldeneye in...New Brunswick. Canadian Wildlife Mgmt. Bulletin series 2(9):1-47.

Chabreck, R.H., 1963. Breeding habits of the pied-billed grebe in...Louisiana Auk 80:447-452.

Chapman, F., 1907. The warblers of North America. D. Appleton and Co., New York 306p.

Connor, R.N, et al., 1975. Woodpecker nesting habitat...in Virginia. J. Wildlife Mgmt. 39(1):144-150.

Cornwell, G.W., 1963. Observations on...Belted kingfishers. Condor 65(5):426-431.

Coulter, M.W., 1957. Food of wood ducks in Maine. J. Wildlife Mgmt. 21(2):235-236,

Coulter, M.W. & Miller, W.R., 1968. Nesting biology of black ducks and mallards in...New England. Vermont Fish & Game Dept. Bull. 68(2):1-74.

Craighead, J., and Craighead, F., 1969. Hawks, owls, and wildlife. Dover Publ., New York 443p.

Earhart, C.M., and Johnson, N.K., 1970. Size dimorphism...of N. American owls. Condor 72(3):251-264.

Ellison, L.N., 1971. Territoriality in spruce grouse. Auk 88:652-664.

1973. Seasonal social organization...spruce grouse. Condor 75:375-385.

Erickson, A.B., 1941. A study of Wilson's snipe. Wilson Bull. 53(1):62.

Errington, P.L., & McDonald, M., 1937. Food habits of Iowa barred owls. Iowa Bird Life. 7:47-49.

Erskine, A.J., 1971. Buffleheads. Canadian Wildl. Serv. Monogr. No. 4. 240p.

Faaborg, J., 1976. Habitat selection...of small grebes of North Dakota. Wilson Bull. 88(3):390-399.

Fitch, H.S., et. al., 1946. Behavior...of red-tailed hawks. Condor. 48:205-237.

Fogarty, M.J., & Arnold, K.A., 1977. Common snipe. Pp. 180-209. Mgmt. of Migratory Shore & Upland Game Birds in N. America. IAFWA, Wash. D.C. 358p.

Forbush, E.H., 1929. Birds of...New England States. Mass Dept. of Agric. Vol. 1, Vol. 2, Vol. 3.

Forbush, E.H. and May, J.B., 1939. Natural History of...N. American Birds. Houghton Mifflin Co., Boston. 554p.

Fredrickson, L.H., 1970. Breeding biology of American coots in Iowa. Wilson Bull. 82(4):445-457.
   1971. Common gallinule...development. Auk 88(4):914-919.
   1977. American coot. Pp. 123-147. Mgmt. of Migratory Shore & Upland Game Birds in N. America. IAFWA 358p.

Fritz, R.S., 1977. The spruce grouse in the Adirondacks. The Conservationist 31(4):19-22.

Gates, J.M., 1972. Red-tailed hawk...in Wisconsin. Wilson Bull. 84:421-433.

Glover, F.A., 1953. Nesting ecology of pied-billed grebe in...Iowa. Wilson Bull. 65(1):32-39.

Goodwin, D., 1976. Crows of the world. Cornell Univ. Press, Ithaca, N.Y. 359p.

Graber, J.W., et. al., 1972. Illinois birds: Hirundinidae. Ill. Nat. Hist. Survey...80. 36p.
   1973. Illinois birds: Laniidae. Ill. Nat. Hist. Survey...83. 18p.
   1977. Illinois birds: Picidae. Ill. Nat. Hist. Survey...102. 73p.

Grice, D., and Rogers, J.P., 1965. The wood duck in Mass. Final Rep. Fed. Aid in Wildl. Restor. Proj. W-19-R. 96p.

Griscom, L., 1937. A monographic study of the red crossbill. Proc. of the Boston Soc. of Nat. Hist. 41:77-210.

Griscom, L., and Sprunt, A., Jr., 1957. Warblers of America. Devin-Adair Co., N.Y. 356p.

Gullion, G.W., 1953. Territorial behavior of the American coot. Condor 55(4): 169-186.
   1972. Improving your forested lands for ruffed grouse. Publ. No. 1439. Misc. Jour. Series Minn. Agr. Exp. Sta. 34p.

Hagar, D.C., Jr., 1957. Nesting populations of red-tailed hawks and horned owls in...New York. Wilson Bull. 69:263-272.

Hammond, D.E., and Wood, R.L., 1977. New Hampshire and the disappearing loon. Loon Preservation Committee, Meredith, N.H. 16p.

Harlow, R.C., 1922. The breeding habits of the northern raven in Pennsylvania. Auk 39:399-410.

Hausman, L.A., 1966. Birds of prey of northeastern N. America. R.R. Smith, Publ., Peterborough, New Hampshire. 164p.

Hays, H., 1972. Polyandry in the spotted sandpiper. Living Bird 11:43-57.

Hecht, W.R., 1951. Nesting of the marsh hawk at Delta, Manitoba. Wilson Bull. 63:167-176.

Hester, F.E., and Dermid., J., 1973. The world of the wood duck. Lippincott Co., N.Y. 160p.

Hochbaum, H.A., 1944. The canvasback on a prairie marsh. Wildl. Mgmt. Inst., Wash., D.C. 201p.

Hooper, R.G., 1977. Nesting habitat of common ravens in Virginia. Wilson Bull. 89(2):233-242.

Hoyt, S.F., 1957. The ecology of the pileated woodpecker. Ecology 38(2):246-256.

James, R.D., 1976. Foraging behavior...of vireos in southern Ontario. Wilson Bull. 88:62-75.

Johnsgard, P.A., 1975. Waterfowl of N. America. Indiana Univ. Press, Bloomington. 575p.

Johnston, D.W., 1961. The biosystematics of American crows. U. of Washington Press, Seattle. 119p.

Jurek, R.M., and Leach, H.R., 1977. Shorebirds. Pp 301-320. Mgmt. of Migratory Shore & Upland Game Birds in N. America. IAFWA, 358p.

Kempton, R.M., 1927. Notes on...turkey vultures. Wilson Bull. 39(3):142-145.

Kendeigh, S.C., 1945. Nesting behavior of wood warblers. Wilson Bull. 57:145-164.

Kushlan, J.A., 1976. Feeding behavior of North American herons. Auk 93(1):86-94.

Lanyon, W.E., 1957. The comparative biology of the meadowlarks in Wis. Publ. of Nuttall Ornith. Club. No. 1 Cambridge, Mass. 67p.

Lawrence, L. De K., 1947. Five days with pair of nesting Canada jays. Canadian Field Nat. 61:1-12.
   1949. The red crossbill...Ontario. Can. Field Nat. 63:147-160.

Low, J.B., 1945. Ecology...of the redhead, in Iowa. Ecol. Monogr. 15:35-69.

MacArthur, R.H., 1958. Population ecology of some warblers of...coniferous forests. Ecology 39(4):599-619.

Mendall, H.L., 1937. Nesting of the bay-breasted warbler. Auk. 54:429-439.
   1944. Food of hawks and owls in Maine. J. Wildl. Mgmt. 8:198-208.
   1958. The ring-necked duck in the Northeast. Univ. Maine Press Orono. 317p.

Mendall, H.L., and Aldous, C.M., 1943. The ecology...of the American woodcock. Maine Coop. Wildl. Res. Unit, Orono. 201p.

Miller, A.B., 1931. Systematic revision and natural history of the American shrikes. Univ. of Calif. Publ. in Zool. 38(2):11-242.

Miller, J.R., and Miller, J.T., 1948. Nesting of the spotted sandpiper at Detroit. Auk 65(4):558-567.

Morse, D.H., 1976. Variables affecting...breeding spruce-wood warblers. Ecology 57(2):290-301.

Mosby, H.S., and Handley, C.O., 1943. The wild turkey in Virginia. Va. Comm. Game & Inland Fisheries, Richmond. 281p.

Murray, J.J., 1940. Nesting habits of the raven in Rockbridge County, Virginia. Raven 20:40-43.

Nickell, W.P., 1943. Observations on the nesting of the killdeer. Wilson Bull. 55:23-28.

Noble, G.K., et. al., 1938. Social behavior of the black-crowned night heron. Auk 55:7-40.

Odum, R.R., 1977. Sora. 57-65. Mgmt. of Migratory Shore & Upland Game Birds in N. America. IAFWA, Wash., D.C. 358p.

Ogden, J.C., 1975. Effects of bald eagle territoriality on nesting ospreys. Wilson Bull. 87(4):496-505.

Orians, G.H., and Kuhlman, F., 1956. Red-tailed hawk and horned owl populations in Wis. Condor 58:371-385.

Owen, R.B., Jr., 1977. American woodcock. Pp. 150-186. Mgmt. of Migratory Shore & Upland Game Birds in N. America. IAFWA, Wash., D.C. 358p.

Palmer, R.S., 1962. Handbook of N. American birds. Vol. I. Loons through flamingos. Yale Univ. Press, New Haven. 567p.
1976. Handbook of N. American birds. Vols. 2 and 3. Waterfowl. Yale Univ. Press, New Haven.

Payne, R.B., 1983. Distributional checklist of birds of Michigan. Museum of Zoology, Univ. of Michigan, Ann Arbor.

Petersen, A.J., 1955. The breeding cycle in the bank swallow. Wilson Bull. 67(4):235-286.

Peterson, R.T., 1980. A Field Guide to the Birds. Houghton Mifflin Company, Boston.

Platt, J.B., 1976. Sharp-shinned hawk...in Utah. Condor 78(1):102.

Pough, R.H., 1951. Audubon water bird guide. Doubleday & Co., Inc., New York. 352p.

Pratt, H.M., 1970. Breeding...of great blue herons & common egrets in...Calif. Condor 72:407-416.

Prince, H.H., 1968. Nest sites used by wood ducks and common goldeneyes in New Brunswick. J. Wildl. Mgmt. 32:489-500.

Randall, B.E., 1940. Seasonal food habits of the marsh hawk in Penn. Wilson Bull. 52:165-172.

Raynor, G.S., 1941. The nesting habits of the whip-poor-will. Bird-banding 12:98-104.

Roest, A.I., 1957. Notes on the American sparrow hawk. Auk 74(1):1-19.

Roseberry, J.L., and Klimstra, W.D., 1970. The nesting ecology...of the eastern meadowlark. Wilson Bull. 82(3):243-267.

Rosene, W., 1969. The bobwhite quail. Rutgers Univ. Press, New Brunswick, New Jersey. 418p.

Sayler, J.C., and Lagler, K.F., 1946. The eastern belted kingfisher in...fish management. Trans. Am. Fisheries Soc. 76th Ann. Meet. 97-117pp.

Schorger, A.W., 1966. The wild turkey. Univ. of Okla. Press, Norman, 625p.

Sheldon, W.G., 1967. The book of the American woodcock. Univ. of Mass. Press, Amherst. 227p.

Simpson, M.B., Jr., 1969. The prothonotary warbler in the Carolina Piedmont. Chat. 33(2):31-37.

Smith, D.G., et. al., 1972. The biology of the American kestrel in...Utah. Southwest Nat. 17(1):73-83.

Stenger, J., and Falls, J.B., 1959. The utilized territory of the ovenbird. Wilson Bull. 71:125-140.

Stewart, P.A., 1952. Dispersed breeding behavior...of banded barn owls in N. America. Auk 69:227-245.

Stewart, R.E., and Kantrud, H.A., 1972. Population estimates of breeding birds in North Dakota. Auk 89(4):766-788.

Stoddard, H.L., 1931. The bobwhite quail. C. Scribner's and Sons, New York. 559p.

Stotts, V., 1957. The black duck in...Chesapeake Bay. Proc. 10th Ann. Conf., Southeastern Assoc. of Game and Fish Comm. 234-242pp.

Strohmeyer, D.L., 1977. Common gallinule. 110-117pp. Mgmt. of Migratory & Upland Game Birds in N. America. IAFWA, Wash. D.C., 358p.

Svoboda, F.J., and Gullion, G.W., 1972. Preferential use of aspen by ruffed grouse in northern Minnesota. J. Wildlife Mgmt. 36:1166-1180.

Tanner, W.D., Jr., and Hendrickson, G.O., 1956. Ecology of the sora in...Iowa. Iowa Bird Life 26(4):78-81.

Thompson, C.F., and Nolan, V., Jr., 1973. Population biology of the yellow-breasted chat in southern Indiana. Ecol. Monogr. 43:145-171.

Todd, W.E.C., 1940. Birds of western Pennsylvania. Univ. of Pittsburgh Press. 710p.

Tuck, L.M., 1972. The snipes. Can. Wildl. Serv. Monogr. 5. 428p.

Tyrrell, W.B., 1945. A study of the northern raven. Auk 62:1-7.

Van Camp, L.F., and Henny, C.J., 1975. The screech owl...in n. Ohio. N. Am. Fauna No. 71. U.S. Fish and Wildl. Serv. 65p.

Vermeer, K., 1973. Some aspects...of common loons in Alberta. Wilson Bull. 85(4):429-435.

Walkinshaw, L.H., 1938. Nesting studies of the pro-thonotary warbler. Bird-Banding 9:32-46.
1940. Summer life of the sora rail. Auk 57:153-168.
1953. Life history of the prothonotary warbler. Wilson Bull. 5: 152-168.
1957. Yellow-bellied flycatcher nesting in Michigan. Auk 74:293-304.
1973. Cranes of the World. Winchester Press N.Y.

Walkinshaw, L.H., and Wolf, A.M., 1957. Distribu-tion of the palm warbler...in Michigan. Wilson Bull. 69:338-351.

Wallace, G.J., 1948. The barn owl in Michigan. Mich. State Col. Agric. Exp. Tech. Bull. No. 208.

Webster, C.G., 1964. Fall foods of soras...in Con-necticut. J. Wildl. Mgmt. 28(1):163-165.

White, H.C., 1953. The eastern belted kingfisher in the Maritime Provinces. Bull. 97, Fisheries Res. Board of Canada, Ottawa. 44p.

White, M., and Harris, S., 1966. Winter occur-rence...of snipe in northwest California. J. Wildl. Mgmt. 30(1):23-34.

Wiens, J.A., 1969. An approach to ecological rela-tionships among grassland birds. Am. Ornith. Union. Ornith. Monogr. No. 8. 93p.

Willoughby, E.J., and Kape, T.J., 1964. Breeding behavior of the American kestrel. The Living Bird. 3:75-96.

Work, T.H., and Wool, A.J., 1942. The nest life of the turkey vulture. Condor 44:145-159.